THE
UNFAILING
LOVE *of* JESUS

R. T. KENDALL

Charisma
HOUSE
A STRANG COMPANY

Most STRANG COMMUNICATIONS/CHARISMA HOUSE/SILOAM/ FRONTLINE/EXCEL BOOKS/REALMS products are available at special quantity discounts for bulk purchase for sales promotions, premiums, fund-raising, and educational needs. For details, write Strang Communications/Charisma House/Siloam/FrontLine/ Excel Books/Realms, 600 Rinehart Road, Lake Mary, Florida 32746, or telephone (407) 333-0600.

THE UNFAILING LOVE OF JESUS by R. T. Kendall
Published by Charisma House
A Strang Company
600 Rinehart Road
Lake Mary, Florida 32746
www.charismahouse.com

Unless otherwise noted, all Scripture quotations are from the Holy Bible, New International Version. Copyright © 1973, 1978, 1984, International Bible Society. Used by permission.

Scripture quotations marked CEV are from the Contemporary English Version, copyright © 1995 by the American Bible Society. Used by permission.

Scripture quotations marked KJV are from the King James Version of the Bible.

Scripture quotations marked NAS are from the New American Standard Bible. Copyright © 1960, 1962, 1963, 1968, 1971, 1972, 1973, 1975, 1977 by the Lockman Foundation. Used by permission. (www.Lockman.org)

Design Director: Bill Johnson
Cover Designer: Judith McKittrick
Cover Illustration: © Tim Teebken, Photodisc

Library of Congress Cataloging-in-Publication Data:
Kendall, R. T.
  The unfailing love of Jesus / R.T. Kendall.
    p. cm.
  ISBN 978-1-59979-228-6
  1. Jesus Christ--Person and offices--Biblical teaching. 2. Love--
Biblical teaching. 3. Christian life--Biblical teaching. 4. Martha,
Saint. 5. Mary, of Bethany, Saint. I. Title.

BT205.K435 2008
232--dc22

                    2007052283

This book was previously published as *Does Jesus Care?* by Paternoster
Press, ISBN 0-85364-776-3, in 1997, and originally published by
Hodder and Stoughton Religious, copyright © 1986.

08 09 10 11 12 — 987654321
Printed in the United States of America

To Marilyn

CONTENTS

PREFACE

Lord, don't you care?" Martha's question to Jesus in Luke 10:40 verbalizes what all of us have felt at one time or another about God. It is interesting that the Lord was not offended by what Martha felt, but it is more interesting that Jesus had His own point of view on the matter. So it is every time we ask the question, "Does Jesus care?"

I take deepest pleasure in dedicating this book to my own sister, Marilyn, who lives in Atlanta, Georgia. Marilyn was only two years old when our mother died in 1953. Several weeks later I myself moved to Tennessee to begin my academic training, and contacts with her have been far from frequent over the years. Both of us have wondered many times why God allowed things to happen as they did concerning us. This book seeks to answer such questions.

I wish to thank Miss Carolyn Armitage of Hodder and Stoughton for the encouragement she has given me in the writing of this book, not to mention her invaluable suggestions. I appreciate the help given by Mrs. Kim Bush, and I want to thank Mrs. Doris Midgley for typing the original manuscript from the sermons I preached at Westminster Chapel during the autumn of 1985. This present book has been completely rewritten, however, and this is minimal reference to the original preaching.

—R. T. KENDALL
www.rtkendallministries.com

INTRODUCTION

Do you know the feeling of being completely let down by the one you thought was the only person who could help you? Have you had this happen in the hour of your greatest need? Do you know the feeling of being deserted by your best friend? It may have been a parent, or a brother or sister, or your closest confidant and advisor. In any case, it was your last resort, if not your only one, and you discovered that your friend's response to your plea was hardly what you expected. You were left in a state of dismay and bewilderment. You had to conclude that this person, difficult though it was to accept, didn't care.

But what if that last resort was Jesus? Surely He cares. When men fail, Jesus is always there. He never fails. He not only cares, but He also can do anything. He has the power to heal, lift depression, cast out demons, and multiply five loaves of bread and two fish into enough food to feed thousands. Jesus can do that—even without being physically present.

So Mary and Martha thought. These two sisters were concerned about their brother, Lazarus, who lay dying. The three of them had one thing in common: they knew and loved Jesus and were sure that Jesus knew and loved them. When Lazarus first became ill, they probably did not worry too much. People become sick and then get better all the time. At any rate, if Lazarus got worse, they could send word to Jesus.

Lazarus indeed got worse, so the word the sisters sent said, "Lord, the one you love is sick" (John 11:3). Jesus was their only resort. It did not cross their minds that Jesus would let them down in their hour of need. What is more, they got the important message to Him in time for Jesus either to "say the word" from where He was and heal by remote control as He had done before (Matt. 8:13), or to come in person and heal Lazarus.

To their shock and devastating disappointment, Jesus did neither. Lazarus died. Jesus showed up after the funeral. "Lord," Martha said to Jesus, "if you had been here, my brother would not have died" (John 11:21). Mary later repeated exactly the same words to Him with undisguised bitterness (John 11:32).

It is one thing to have a trusted, earthly friend let us down, and quite another to have Jesus do it. That is what Jesus did. So they thought, and so it seemed at the time.

"Does Jesus care?" was probably what they began to think during the waiting period as Lazarus's condition grew worse. "Does Jesus care?" they must have asked during the funeral. How could He desert them at such a time? What had they done to deserve this? Had they unwittingly offended Jesus at some point along the way? Were they wrong to lay their need before Him? Were they being presumptuous? Were they taking advantage of what they thought was a special relationship? Were they wrong in actually thinking He cared?

The one thing of which they had no doubt was Jesus's power to heal. It never crossed their minds to question His ability. Could His refusal to heal Lazarus really have been deliberate?

Jesus instead sent a cryptic message to Mary and Martha that no doubt gave them considerable encouragement: "This sickness will not end in death. No, it is for God's glory so that God's Son may be glorified through it" (John 11:4). That encouragement probably lasted until the moment Lazarus expired. Then bewilderment set in, and they were trying to grasp the meaning of it all. Nothing added up.

Are you trying to understand God's way? Perhaps it concerns the death of someone you prayed for. Or a condition you asked God to prevent. Or the betrayal by a friend whom you considered to be the one and only person you trusted. Or a financial matter you prayed over, only to have things go from bad to worse. Perhaps it was a failure to have presence of mind in a situation about which you had prayed earnestly in advance. Or a feeling of rejection by God when the momentous occasion that you looked forward to finally came. Did you have an accident despite praying for traveling mercies? Did you feel a loss of protection despite earnest praying? Perhaps the job you dreamed of and prayed for fell through. Or was it a collapse of plans after considerable prayer?

Does Jesus care? How can anyone think He cares when He doesn't answer prayer that is put to Him in adequate time? Am I to believe that Jesus cares for me when He hears my cry and does nothing?

Yes. That is the answer, and it is the correct one. It is not wishful thinking that supplies the positive answer to the "Does Jesus care?" question asked in this book. It is the absolute true answer. I ask the reader carefully to follow the account of Jesus's response to Mary and Martha as it is found in John 11. We make a hasty conclusion, not to mention the wrong one, if we say He does not care. This book will not only show that Jesus cares but also that He cares more deeply and painstakingly than you or I can begin to imagine.

This book does not seek to prove God's power to do anything. That is assumed from the outset. This book may or may not be of benefit to the reader who questions God's ability. There is a place for a book demonstrating God's power, but this is not it. I come to the reader simply with the conviction that nothing is too hard for the Lord (Jer. 32:27) and that nothing is impossible with God (Luke 1:37).

The purpose of this book is to show something of God's hidden ways. They are revealed in the person of Jesus, who was God on Earth and is eternally God in heaven. "In the beginning was the Word, and the Word was with God, and the Word was God" (John 1:1). Jesus was God in the flesh (John 1:14). He was man as though He were not God, yet God as though He were not man. Thus all Jesus was on Earth was a mirror of the true and only God in all His ways.

> Does Jesus care when my heart is pained
> Too deeply for mirth or song;
> As the burdens press, and the cares distress
> And the way grows early and long?
>
> Does Jesus care when my way is dark
> With a nameless dread and fear?
> As the daylight fades into deep night shades,
> Does He care enough to be near?

Does Jesus care when I've tried and failed
To resist some temptation strong;
When for my deep grief there is no relief,
Though my tears flow all the night long?

Does Jesus care when I've said "goodbye"
To the dearest on earth to me,
And my sad heart aches till it nearly breaks,
Is it aught to Him? Does He see?

Oh yes, He cares, I know He cares,
His heart is touched with my grief;
When the days are weary, the long nights dreary,
I know my Savior cares.[1]
—FRANK E. GRAEFF

Does Jesus care? Yes, He cares. Because God cares.

1

DOES JESUS CARE WHEN WE ARE UNWELL?

I t may seem odd to ask, "Does Jesus care when we are unwell?" in the light of the many healings He enabled when He was on the earth. But it was precisely this question Lazarus must have asked when Jesus did not come straightaway to heal him. It is, in fact, the way we all feel when we are unwell.

If I have an illness worse than a headache, I almost always take it to the Lord in prayer. I know what it is to be unwell. A few weeks after Louise and I married, a growth on my right leg was diagnosed as possible cancer. Prayer ascended to heaven on my behalf, but things got worse. I was put in the hospital, and the growth was surgically removed. The biopsy showed that it was in a premalignant stage.

When I was a pastor in Fort Lauderdale, I was taken to the hospital for what was thought to be a heart attack. I was in intensive care for several days. Many prayed for me. It was shortly revealed that I had gallstones—the symptoms simulating a heart attack. I was advised that the gallbladder must be removed. We prayed. There was no healing. The gallbladder was removed.

To my knowledge, I have never been healed except for what could be explained medically. A possible exception to this was when I was five years old. Because I was born with a double hernia, my parents called in a saintly woman who anointed me and prayed for my healing. The condition eventually disappeared, so this might be the exception. But in my adult life, I do not recall any incident by which I could claim to have been healed.

Neither do I know of a case in which my own prayer for another resulted in healing. I have wished for the gift of healing (1 Cor. 12:9) and have taken courage from Paul's urging that we "eagerly desire" the best gifts (1 Cor. 12:31). As of now, my desire remains unfulfilled. I have concluded, perhaps wrongly, that I could not be trusted with such a gift. In any case, I believe that it is God's will for the gifts of the Spirit to be present in the church and that Jesus Christ is no less able to heal today than He was more than two thousand years ago (Heb. 13:8).

The closest I have personally come to a rather unusual incident bordering on healing involved my wife. A number of years ago, an unpretentious but remarkable man came to our house for dinner. We knew that he claimed to have seen some manifestations of healing in his work in Fort Lauderdale, but my wife, for some reason, asked me *not* to say anything to him about her jaw. For several weeks a condition developed that made it almost impossible for her to open her mouth.

She could barely open it enough to eat a piece of meat. Our doctor was not sure what the cause was but thought her going into the hospital for an operation was the only hope.

While spending an evening with our friend, I longed to tell him about Louise's problem. At eleven o'clock, he was walking toward the door with his briefcase in hand when I blurted, "Louise, please let me tell him about your jaw." He turned to her and asked, "What's the problem?" She then explained. He set his briefcase on the floor, put his hand on her jaw, and said, "In the name of Jesus, be healed. Now open your jaw." She opened it wide without any pain and exclaimed, "I'm healed!" Our friend picked up his briefcase and said good-bye as though nothing unusual had taken place.

A WORD FROM GOD

"...This sickness will not end in death. No, it is for God's glory so that God's Son may be glorified through it" (John 11:4). Jesus never healed Lazarus but sent a word instead. When we are unwell, especially if we develop much pain or distress, we are likely to call on God for help. Sometimes He responds with a word. The difficulty we often face is that of either misinterpreting that word or hastily applying it according to our personal wish. In the case of Lazarus and his sisters, we cannot be absolutely sure what their thoughts were when Jesus gave them a specific word. But they must have thought that Lazarus would be healed.

When we are desperately in need of encouragement, we are extremely vulnerable to any number of suggestions. For example: If a person is very hungry, he will look anywhere—even in the garbage can—for food. When a person is bereaved, he will often accept comfort from any source. The cultists often prey on bereaved people in order to spread their errors. When we are vulnerable, even *the very Word of God* can be misunderstood. For when we are grasping for hope, any word—even God's Word—can be falsely applied.

God may choose to speak in a number of different ways when we are discouraged. We may hear Him through reading the Bible, preaching, singing, or being around Christian friends. Most of us have tried "the lucky dip," as one of our friends put it, namely opening the Bible at random for a direct word from God. I admit to having done this, and I do not deny that God has—infrequently—spoken to me in this manner. God is gracious, especially to young Christians. But beware of this approach. The devil can get in when we are vulnerable.

There is an old story that bears repeating: A distraught person decided to turn to the Bible at random to get a quick word from God. She opened to these words, "And Judas went out and hanged himself." Distressed at this, she tried again. Her eyes fell on the words, "Go, and do thou likewise." By now she was in a state of sheer panic but decided to give it one more try. She turned to the words, "What thou doest, do quickly." I can tell you that I have had similar experiences when I have turned to the Bible in this Russian-roulette manner.

More often than not I find that God speaks to me through my daily Bible reading. I personally use Robert Murray M'Cheyne's plan, by which one can read through the Bible in one year, two years, or four years. On countless occasions

I have known God to speak powerfully to me in my normal course of daily reading. It can happen through a word "leaping up off the page," or in a very quiet, unsensational but real manner. Yet, even then, one must be careful not to be hasty in applying such a word from God.

I can remember one occasion when I *knew* that God Himself had given me a definite word, but I didn't know what to make of it. I shared it with my wife. To her the meaning was obvious, and she showed me what it meant to her and what it must surely mean to me at that moment. She was right. The consequence of the way she was able to apply that word to me was one of the greatest, life-changing experiences I have ever had. But at the time, I was so depressed that I could not see the obvious.

God can speak to us, but it does not always follow that our immediate interpretation is the correct one.

But how do we know if it is from God? *Peace.* God's Word gives peace. It is a peace that transcends understanding (Phil. 4:7). One may not understand God's Word at first, especially its implications. But the peace testifies that it *is* from Him. And knowing it is from Him is enough.

The word Jesus gave to Lazarus and his sisters was that his particular illness was for God's glory. I cannot imagine a more consoling word. Why? Because this tells me that my illness is unrelated to any personal guilt and that God has the matter in hand.

WHY DID THIS HAPPEN?

When we are unwell, many of us ask God, "Why did You let this happen to me?" Not far away is the ominous thought that God is "getting even" for something we have done that offended Him. After all, who among us cannot think of some sin or fault that God could, if He chose, deal with? But to hear that our illness is for God's glory makes us see straightaway that not only is the matter in hand—God knows all about it and has things under control—but also He is not blaming us.

There is a sense that all illness is for God's glory. On one occasion Jesus encountered a man who was blind from birth. His disciples asked, "'Rabbi, who sinned, this man or his parents, that he was born blind?' 'Neither this man nor his parents sinned,' said Jesus, 'but this happened so that the work of God might be displayed in his life'" (John 9:1–3). In ancient Judaism there was a popular consensus that serious illness was the direct consequence of some heinous sin. This is why many Jews never understood the Book of Job. Job was "...blameless and upright; he feared God and shunned evil" (Job 1:1). When catastrophe struck, leaving him financially and physically broken, his "friends" kept probing Job for some secret sin that they believed lay at the cause. (See Job 22:5.)

It is true that sometimes sin is the cause of sickness. This was implied when Jesus said to a paralytic, "Take heart, son; your sins are forgiven" (Matt. 9:2). For example: Sexual sin can lead to venereal disease. The inability to control one's appetite can lead to being overweight, which in turn can be the cause of any number of diseases—from high blood pressure to heart trouble. Not only that, but also it can be demonstrated that such things as bitterness or holding a grudge can lead to various illnesses, including arthritis.

But the Bible does not teach that every serious illness can be traced to sin. James told us to anoint with oil on behalf of the sick who ask for such, and he promised that the prayer of faith would make them well. But he added, "...If he has sinned, he will be forgiven" (James 5:15). This suggests that illness *may* be the consequence of sin. But the word *if* categorically proves that such a person may *not* have sinned and still be unwell.

Several summers ago we were vacationing in Key Largo, Florida. Some friends offered us the use of their own home while they themselves spent part of the summer in Iowa. My family and I had looked forward to that time with no small anticipation. During our first week, my wife suddenly became very ill. She could not hold any food down, and we had to take her to the doctor. In the meantime, we prayed most earnestly, only to discover she was getting worse. At one point it looked as though we would have to put her in the hospital to keep her from dehydrating. She lost weight before the ordeal passed.

Why did God let it happen? I can't be sure. But Louise decided to take advantage of the loss of weight and hasn't regained it. She felt she needed to lose all that weight anyway, and perhaps it was the only way it could happen. Since then, she has never felt better!

It may be that all of us should try to trace the rainbow through the rain when illness persists. It may be a small thing or a large thing that we need to discover. But as Christians we can always affirm illness to be for God's glory. God has a purpose in what He permits. "And we know that all things work together for good to them that love God, to them who are the called according to *his* purpose" (Rom. 8:28, KJV, emphasis added).

When we are unwell, whether from flu, migraine, or whatever, our hasty reaction is that Jesus does not care—especially if we don't get well soon. But sometimes things must get worse before they can get better. And, almost always, we have to wait awhile before we can assess God's purpose objectively. I can promise this: sooner or later not only will you see that Jesus cares, but also the end result of the ordeal will be more glorious than the immediate result you wanted.

God shows that He cares when *He* gives us an undoubted word in our time of illness. The worst thing that can happen to an individual or a nation is God's utter silence. The prophet Amos once predicted that God would send a famine through the land: "...not a famine of food or a thirst for water, but a famine of hearing the words of the LORD" (Amos 8:11). Such is the greatest possible famine for a nation; it is when one simply cannot find a place where the gospel is being preached, where there is no faithful exposition of the Word, or where no voice that truly speaks for God can be found. This can happen at the individual level. King Saul lamented, "...God has turned away from me. He no longer answers me, either by prophets or by dreams..." (1 Sam. 28:15).

But when God speaks in a definite way, it is proof that He cares. He therefore showed His care for Lazarus and his sisters by giving them a word, even if they did not grasp all that Jesus meant by it.

Healing...Now or Later

And yet, sometimes God shows that He cares by healing the person right on the spot. I have known dozens of cases in which divine healing took place. "Jesus Christ is the same yesterday and today and forever" (Heb. 13:8). As surely as Jesus lives today and is reigning from the right hand of God the Father, we may believe that He will heal. We should never be surprised at the miraculous. Jesus promised, "I tell you the truth, anyone who has faith in me will do what I have been doing. He will do even greater things than these, because I am going to the Father. And I will do whatever you ask in my name, so that the Son may bring glory to the Father" (John 14:12–13).

I am sure that one of the reasons we do not see more of the miraculous is merely because we neither ask for it nor expect it. James said, "...You do not have, because you do not ask God" (James 4:2).

> O what peace we often forfeit,
> O what needless pain we bear,
> All because we do not carry
> Everything to God in prayer.[1]
>
> —Joseph M. Scriven

Who knows what God might do? The king of Nineveh took seriously Jonah's prophecy that in forty days Nineveh would be destroyed. The king proclaimed a fast and hoped. "Who knows?" he asked. "God may yet relent and with compassion turn from his fierce anger so that we will not perish" (Jon. 3:9).

When there is illness, we should pray. We should turn to God. We should turn to Him who once promised, "Call to me and I will answer you and tell you great and unsearchable things you do not know" (Jer. 33:3). This was the word to Jeremiah, to whom God had previously said, "I am the LORD, the God of all mankind. Is anything too hard for me?" (Jer. 32:27).

What if Lazarus and his two sisters had not turned to Jesus at all? Not only would they have missed a word from Him (John 11:4), but also they would never have known the full extent of God's purpose for them in this situation. Never conclude that any matter—be it illness or any kind of a problem—should not be taken to the Lord. It will follow as a consequence of turning to Him that we shall be able to explore His love and purpose in greater depths.

FEAR OF REJECTION

The reason we don't turn to God as we should is partly owing to the fear of being rejected. The fear of rejection can be a very powerful, but always negative, force in our lives. I know many young men who are lonely but will not invite a Christian lady to spend an evening out with them for one reason: the fear of rejection.

The fear of rejection can be paralyzing and so inhibiting that we can become warped in our personalities. With Jesus there is total acceptance, even with our weaknesses (Heb.

4:15). "For no matter how many promises God has made, they are 'Yes' in Christ…" (2 Cor. 1:20). God does not reject us. He will answer. His answer will be in total love and compassion and totally right. Our very turning to Him will open the way to His higher purpose for us.

Our Lord shows that He cares by bringing us into a caring community. What it must have meant to Lazarus that there were two who cared enough for him to get a word to Jesus on his behalf! One of the ways Jesus shows that He cares is by surrounding us with those who will intercede for us. One of the fringe benefits of being a Christian is Christian fellowship. Once you become a Christian, you are brought into an entirely new family. Your new family will love you in a way that your natural family may not have loved you.

I have watched people from all over the world come to Christ. I have seen many who have come to Him with no Christian background whatsoever. What they could not have known when they first came to Him in faith was that they were getting far more than mere assurance that they would go to heaven when they died. They were getting a new family. I have watched this happen again and again. Those outside the fellowship of the church discover friends inside who become closer than any brother or sister or parent they have ever known. Jesus shows He cares for you by bringing your need to God on your behalf.

If someone who has prayed for you does not get the immediate results sought, remember that this is how it was with Mary and Martha, who interceded on behalf of Lazarus. Do not hold it against the Marys and Marthas of your acquaintance if they don't succeed at first in securing the desired response. But you may be sure that the Lord will give them a word of peace that can be transmitted to you. The Lord will not let *them* down—or *you.*

The delays we experience in getting our exact prayers answered can be painful. But they are painful for our Lord too. Don't you know that it took a perfect faith and total devotion to His Father for Jesus to obey the Father? Don't you know that Jesus wanted to go to Lazarus immediately? Of course He did. He knew what they would feel when He did not come straightaway. He knew the thoughts they would have.

But Jesus was governed by a high principle. "...I tell you the truth, the Son can do nothing by himself; he can do only what he sees his Father doing, because whatever the Father does the Son also does" (John 5:19). Jesus loved Lazarus (John 11:3). But He loved the Father more: "...I seek not to please myself but him who sent me" (John 5:30).

I do not doubt that when Jesus heard Lazarus was unwell, His immediate impulse was to drop what He was doing and make His way to Bethany where Lazarus was. But before He did that, He did something else: He looked to get the green light from His Father. What He got instead was a word that He sent on to Lazarus and his sisters. He did what He had to do. "For I have come down from heaven not to do my will but to do the will of him who sent me" (John 6:38). Paul said, "For even Christ did not please himself..." (Rom. 15:3). He pleased His Father.

Perhaps you will say, "Then Jesus is *for* me and God is *against* me." Wrong! The Father of Jesus is *our* Father who has "lavished on us" great grace and does so "with all wisdom and understanding" (Eph. 1:8). After all, it was the Father's will that Lazarus was not healed because He had a better idea. Never think that Jesus is working for you and God the Father is working against you. Jesus perpetually accepts us as we are but will intercede according to the will of God. The will of God is infallible. At the end of the day, we will not only be without complaints, but we will also marvel at God's goodness and wisdom—even thanking Him for not doing what we initially wanted!

To Those Who Love God

One of the difficulties we all have to overcome is the way God appears to bless people who (apparently) don't desire to be blessed and to withhold blessing from those who deserve it. Perhaps you know someone who is flourishing at the moment. He (or she) is prospering in health, finances, and career, getting all the openings while you are struggling to make ends meet and also trying to please the Lord in all your ways. What adds to the pain is that the person who is prospering does not seem to care one whit about doing things God's way.

This is nothing new. The psalmist counseled, "Do not fret because of evil men or be envious of those who do wrong; for like the grass they will soon wither, like green plants they will soon die away" (Ps. 37:1–2). The psalmist acknowledged that this sort of problem almost got the best of him: "But as for me, my feet had almost slipped; I had nearly lost my foothold. For I envied the arrogant when I saw the prosperity of the wicked" (Ps. 73:2–3). But he went on to say that he entered God's sanctuary: "…then I understood their final destiny" (Ps. 73:17).

My favorite verse in the Bible is Romans 8:28: "And we know that all things work together for good to them that love God, to them who are the called according to *his* purpose" (KJV, emphasis added). This is a promise that does not apply to everyone. It is a promise to those who love God and who are the called according to His purpose. Rather than envy the arrogant who prosper, we should feel sorry for them. Their end is bleak—very bleak indeed. For those who are constrained to wait on God will be found the promise of blessing. "Since ancient times no one has heard, no ear has perceived, no eye has seen any God besides you, who acts on behalf of those who *wait* for him" (Isa. 64:4, emphasis added).

Jesus might have merely answered Mary and Martha with these words: "This sickness is for God's glory"—full stop. What if the Lord had said that? What if our illness was accompanied by no promise of a happy ending but that it is only for God's glory? What then? Could you live with that? Job said, "Though he slay me, yet will I hope in him" (Job 13:15).

When John Calvin lay dying at the comparatively young age of fifty-five, he was in great pain. He was heard to utter, "O Lord, Thou crushest me, but that it is Thy hand, it is enough." We must be devoted to the glory of God more than our immediate wish. As Jesus did what the Father wanted—and only that—so must we. Paul said, "I know what it is to be in need, and I know what it is to have plenty. I have learned the secret of being content in any and every situation, whether well or hungry, whether living in plenty or in want" (Phil. 4:12).

See the End From the Beginning

God actually got greater glory by not healing Lazarus. Here is the lesson we can deduce from this story: *when God doesn't heal, it is because He has something better in mind.* Whoever you are, dear reader, you might be suffering with some illness or physical problem. It may not be anything serious, but most of us have something or other that is not functioning as it once did. But if we live by the principle of the great glory of God, we can be assured, in advance, that what God finally does with us is better than anything we could have wished for or imagined. Jesus did not tell Lazarus and his sisters what would finally happen. Sometimes God clearly speaks to us but lets us grasp His richer meaning more fully later.

Perhaps Jesus would have preferred to send the details of the promised outcome to Mary and Martha in order to relieve them of anxiety. Perhaps it was not easy for Him to keep the secret to Himself. In any case, our Lord did not spell out to Mary and Martha what He would do eventually. This was further evidence of His perfect faith and total devotion to the Father's will. Perhaps God would share most of His secrets with us if we could be trusted to keep such to ourselves. "The Lord confides in those who fear him . . ." (Ps. 25:14).

Much of Jesus's suffering was from keeping how much He knew in His heart. He knew that He would be crucified—and why. But the implications of this were known to Him alone. When He was summoned to Herod's palace, the king had hoped to see a miracle performed by Jesus. What did Jesus do? Nothing. (See Luke 23:8–9.) He just stood there. That infuriated Herod. But Jesus was taking His cue from the Father. It meant suffering.

Jesus knew the possible disillusionment of His followers when He allowed Himself to be crucified. What would those who had been healed think? What about those who were present when He turned five loaves of bread and two fish into enough food to feed five thousand? When Jesus went to the cross, He told no one why, but, "He humbled himself and became obedient to death—even death on a cross!" (Phil. 2:8). He was never given permission to say, "I'm doing this for you. I'm dying in your place. I'm making atonement for the sins of the world." Instead, He allowed people to think what they would. It too was a part of His suffering.

Our Lord's consolation was keeping His own eye on the ultimate event. What kept Him going, humanly speaking, was knowing all would end well. Otherwise there would be nothing but despair for us all.

This is how He can allow suffering. He sees the end from the beginning, however much it hurts Him to let things happen and watch us weep in our perplexity. He waits that He might later see our joy.

Perhaps God lets some of us become unwell for the very purpose that we will turn to Him. I realize that "crisis" faith is not saving faith. All men tend to cry out to God in trouble and illness. Why not? It may be God's way of trying to reach us. Perhaps illness is the only way He can get our attention. The question, however, is not whether we come through the illness, but whether we acknowledge Him as Savior and Lord when we are well.

There is something more important than the healing of the body, and that is getting right with God. What if you are healed but lose your soul? What kind of favor would that be from God? "For what shall it profit a man, if he shall gain the whole world, and lose his own soul?" (Mark 8:36, KJV). It is far better to get right with God and then die than to get well and, in the end, be eternally and hopelessly lost.

We should therefore see any illness, any adversity, any trouble, or any setback as something that is for the glory of God. If it is God's kind way of trying to get our attention, it shows how much He really cares.

2

DOES JESUS CARE WHEN OUR LOVED ONES DIE?

Several years ago, I would spend about two hours each Saturday with our Pilot Lights, witnessing on the streets in the Westminster and Victoria areas. There we met the real world—I mean the *real* world. Every nation, every color, every class of society was represented in the streets of London—many of whom came to see the changing of the guard at Buckingham Palace. By talking to the people, we got to know what they were feeling, asking, wanting, and seeking. As soon as the people discovered we did not want their money, that there was no gimmick, and that we only wanted to talk about Jesus Christ, we discovered some very interesting things. I would summarize this by saying two things I have learned about people—or rather have had confirmed in the light of what the Bible says about man: all men are self-righteous, and all men feel that God owes them an answer.

To put it another way, people have a chip on their shoulder

about God. They feel God has a lot to answer for. Many are very bitter indeed. "Where was God when I needed Him?" "Why did God let my wife die after our baby was born?" "Why did God let me suffer as I did?"

The story of Jesus and His friend Lazarus is a hint from God about the problems of evil and suffering in the world. I am thinking of famine in Ethiopia, earthquakes in South America, the low standard of living in Calcutta, violence in Northern Ireland, hurricanes in the Gulf states of America, ruthless men taking innocent people hostage in aircraft and airports, and sexual crimes against helpless children.

As a college student in Nashville, Tennessee, I remember taking a theological problem to one of the professors one afternoon. I honestly do not remember what my question was, but I have never forgotten his words on that occasion. He patiently listened to my question and we discussed it, and just before I left his house, he said, "Let me ask you a question. Why did God create man when He knew he would suffer?"

I have sought to understand and answer this question for more than thirty years.

But the question could equally be asked, "Why did God create man when He knew He—God Himself—would suffer?"

Most of us never pose the question from God's point of view. It always seems to come from self-righteous man, who instinctively feels he not only has the right to ask it, but that he also deserves an answer.

Incidentally, the Bible has a word that describes the condition of the heart of the man who puts this question in a self-righteous manner. It is called *rebellion*. Sin is rebellion. It is other things too, of course. It is unbelief. It is pride. It is selfishness. It is hate. It is evil desire. It is the love of money and the pride of life. But all these depictions of the sinfulness of man can be summarized in one word: *rebellion*. Man is in rebellion against God.

It does not appear that way to us at first, of course. To see ourselves as being in the wrong against a God who is perfectly just requires the work of the Holy Spirit. Without the Holy Spirit in us, we can only see things from our own perspective, namely that God could not possibly be just and merciful at the same time.

God has allowed Himself to be misunderstood, even to let us ask the question: does He care?

JESUS'S FRIENDS

When Mary and Martha sent word to Jesus, saying, "Lord, the one You love is sick," they could not have known that they were about to touch on the deepest philosophical, theological problem that ever was—the problem of evil. This is not because they had ingenious, inquiring minds, but because it never occurred to them that Jesus would appear to ignore their request.

They were close friends of Jesus. Although Jesus was not swayed by power and influence (Matt. 22:16), there is no doubt that He had His close friends. Among the Twelve, He had His inner circle—Peter, James, and John. Outside the Twelve it seems that among His very closest friends were Mary, Martha, and Lazarus. Therefore, apart from appealing to Jesus's very compassion for the needy, they felt they were on the "inside," as it were, with Jesus.

But when He stayed behind, they began to feel toward God what everyone by nature feels: "Why, God? How could You do this to me?"

Sometimes God turns His back on His closest friends. Why? Perhaps in case they feel they have a special claim on Him. But God is no respecter of persons (Acts 10:34). His closest friends need to learn this most of all. This is possibly why those closest to Him suffer the most. Abraham was called God's "friend" (Isa. 41:8; James 2:23), but no man went through greater trials than he did.

Therefore if you feel severely tested, regard it as a most high compliment. Consider that God wants to be your friend. Martin Luther, the great reformer of the sixteenth century, used to say that we must know God as an enemy before we can know Him as a friend.

Jesus Christ is God. Jesus is God in the flesh. He was man as though He were not God, and He was God as though He were not man. Jesus therefore mirrors God perfectly. "…Anyone who has seen me has seen the Father…" (John 14:9). "I and the Father are one" (John 10:30). If you want to see into the heart of God, look at Jesus. Watch His every move, and you will see God's every move. Notice His reaction to men, and you get God's reaction to men. Therefore notice how He handled Mary's and Martha's request, and you see God's way of handling suffering in a world He loves.

HE KNOWS EVERYTHING

God knows everything that is going on. We may not think He does. But He does. When Jesus did not immediately come to heal Lazarus, Mary and Martha may have wondered if Jesus actually got the word about Lazarus at all, or whether He got the word in sufficient time to do something about it. Jesus's delay in coming to them may have tempted them to say, "He must not know how ill Lazarus is. Surely He would not let him get worse and worse like this."

The Bible says, "Nothing in all creation is hidden from God's sight. Everything is uncovered and laid bare before the eyes of him to whom we must give account" (Heb. 4:13). God knows *everything* that is going on. The nations to Him are but a drop in a bucket (Isa. 40:15), and He knows the number of the very hairs of our heads (Matt. 10:30). He knows all that is going on, seeing the end from the beginning (Isa. 46:10).

Jesus stayed where He was for two days. Finally He moved in the direction of Bethany. He then told His disciples, "'Our friend Lazarus has fallen asleep; but I am going there to wake him up.' His disciples replied, 'Lord, if he sleeps, he will get better.' Jesus had been speaking of his death, but his disciples thought he meant natural sleep. So then he told them plainly, 'Lazarus is dead'" (John 11:11–14).

In the meantime, Mary and Martha were going through the agony of watching their brother get worse and worse. This to say nothing about how Lazarus himself felt. Perhaps one of them paced back and forth in the house that Jesus Himself had been in many times.

They kept looking out of the window in the direction of the Judaean desert. Surely any moment they would see that familiar figure walking their way. They looked toward the window. They looked back at Lazarus. He was getting weaker and weaker. "This sickness will not end in death," they kept saying to themselves, deriving as much comfort as possible from the Lord's own words.

In disbelief they noticed that Lazarus had stopped breathing. They checked his pulse. They listened carefully for a heartbeat. Nothing. "It can't be true," they said, "but it is. Lazarus is dead." The Lord also spoke this several miles away to the disciples. God knows everything that is going on—everything.

But their distress was, in fact, to bring them closer and closer to real friendship with God—not at a human level, but a spiritual level—the kind of relationship Abraham had with Him. And this kind of relationship cannot come except from suffering—not even with Martha and Mary, close friends though they were to Jesus.

Do you feel that Jesus is your friend but that He has let you down? Did you feel Him near, only to feel suddenly deserted? If so, you will know how Isaiah felt: "Truly you are a God who hides himself..." (Isa. 45:15). What makes the hiding of God's face so painful is that it never comes with advance warning. If only God would whisper in our ear, "By the way, next Tuesday about 2:30 in the afternoon, you just might notice the withdrawal of the light of My countenance. Don't let it worry you. I shall just be hiding My face for a little while." No, God doesn't do it like this—giving warning. He just *does* it.

COME UP HIGHER

But to be treated in this manner is a singular kindness. It is an invitation to "move up higher," to join the ranks of the great saints of old. That is the way they "made it." That is what made them successful. The writer of Hebrews says they did it "by faith."

"Some faced jeers and flogging, while still others were chained and put in prison. They were stoned; they were sawed in two; they were put to death by the sword..." (Heb. 11:36–37). Such people were graced with enormous faith, all because they dignified the trial God gave them. "Blessed is the man who perseveres under trial, because when he has stood the test, he will receive the crown of life that God has promised to those who love him" (James 1:12).

On the morning of April 8, 1953, I received my first invitation (that I can remember) to "come up higher" into God's grace. Eight weeks before, I was called out of class at Ashland High School in Ashland, Kentucky. I went to the principal's office to take a telephone call. My uncle's voice at the end of the line said, "RT, your mother has just had a stroke. She is a very sick woman. Your father is on the way to your school to pick you up and take you with him to see her in the hospital."

For the next eight weeks I nearly froze every time I heard the sound of a telephone. I feared the worst every time. During those eight weeks, my father called every godly person he knew to come in and pray for my mother. She was anointed with oil no fewer than seven times. Two or three well-meaning ladies said that they had "prayed through" on the matter, meaning that God told them my mother would be healed.

One morning I heard my father running up the stairs with

happy laughter. "Wake up, son, your mother is going to be all right."

Groggy but happy to hear this, I climbed out of bed. "How do you know that?" I asked.

"I touched God this morning," my father confidently said. "God gave me a wonderful promise. I know your mother will be healed." I was happy to hear that.

But my mother got worse. One evening I myself thought God told me she would be healed. I came upon a verse of Scripture that, to me, said my mother would be healed. I talked to several people after that moment, telling them that I knew my mother would be healed.

In those days I played in the Ashland High School band. I was an oboist. Our band had been chosen to play at the Cherry Blossom Festival in Washington DC. It was a rare thing for a high school band to be invited to play at the Cherry Blossom Festival. Ours was the only high school in America that was represented at this particular event. The question in the family was whether I should go, seeing that my mother was unwell. All knew how much I had looked forward to this. My mother herself insisted that I go. On Sunday, April 6, I kissed her good-bye.

The train for Washington DC left the next Monday afternoon. After traveling all night, we arrived about seven o'clock Tuesday morning and went into a restaurant to order breakfast. I placed my order, along with some of the students, and then excused myself to call my aunt who lived in Washington DC. I wanted to surprise her and hoped to see her before the day was over. "Where are you?" she asked very curiously.

"I'm at the Pennsylvania Hotel," I said, feeling puzzled that she did not seem in a very good mood.

"Please go back to the hotel right now," she said. "Your Uncle Millard will be there to get you."

"Why?" I asked. "I just arrived."

"He will explain."

"I don't understand," I pleaded.

"He will tell you."

So I began to plead over the phone, "Please tell me what is going on."

Finally my aunt said, "Your mother passed away this morning." My world collapsed. I thought I would die on the spot—at least I wanted to.

I went back to the table in the restaurant and told my friends to cancel my breakfast. "My mother just died," I had to explain to them. But it was my invitation to "move up higher."

My first reaction was that Jesus doesn't care. He gave me His word that my mother would be healed. He gave my dad His word that my mother would be healed. Seven people prayed for her, two or three of whom "prayed through." It was a traumatic experience from which I have never totally recovered.

If Jesus cares when our loved ones die, how does He show it? It is *not* necessarily by stopping our loved ones from dying. All of us will have to die sometime. "For the wages of sin is death" (Rom. 6:23). "Just as man is destined to die once..." (Heb. 9:27). We may therefore assume that our Lord is not going to show that He cares by healing everyone and letting them live on and on. They will eventually have to die, and when should we be willing to give them up?

THIS IS WHY JESUS CAME

And yet the reason Jesus came into the world was to give us eternal life. His death on the cross was to destroy the works of the devil (1 John 3:8), even to "... destroy him who holds the power of death—that is, the devil" (Heb. 2:14). But this victory over Satan was in fact a twofold process, guaranteed by the two comings of Jesus.

When Jesus came to the earth the first time, it was to die on the cross for our sins—but also to ensure Satan's ultimate defeat. After His resurrection, Jesus ascended to the right hand of God where He "must reign until he has put all his enemies under his feet. The last enemy to be destroyed is death" (1 Cor. 15:25–26). This will happen when "the Lord himself will come down from heaven, with a loud command, with the voice of the archangel and with the trumpet call of God, and the dead in Christ will rise first" (1 Thess. 4:16). Those living at the time will be the only ones exempt from having to die. They will be "caught up" to meet the Lord in the air (v. 17).

At some stage after this event, Satan himself will be "thrown into the lake of burning sulfur..." to be "... tormented day and night for ever and ever" (Rev. 20:10). From then on, "There will be no more death or mourning or crying or pain..." (Rev. 21:4). This is why Jesus came.

It would therefore be wrong for us to say the Lord does not care when He does not stop our loved ones from dying.

Even if He should heal them and give them a "reprieve" from immediate death, should we be any more willing to say good-bye to them five or ten or twenty years later? It is not unlikely that when the same loved one who was healed comes to the brink of death again that we would seek the Lord for healing. Of course! And God may heal. But sooner or later we must give them up.

Sergei Nikolaev, a Baptist minister from Leningrad, was my translator on our two-week visit to what was the USSR in 1985. He told me about his grandmother, who became seriously ill at the age of ninety. She asked Sergei to pray for her and anoint her with oil. He did this, and, lo and behold, she was healed quite suddenly and miraculously. The doctor had left the house the night before with the word that the lady would not last two more days. But she was healed. Seven years later, she became ill again. She called for Sergei and said, "Today I go home. Do not pray." She did go home in a few hours, leaving behind a prayer list of five hundred people whom she prayed for by name every day.

When God heals a loved one who is dying, it is probably for one of three reasons. First, because those who would be left behind simply could not cope alone. God knows when this is the case. We all think it may be true with us. But there comes a time when one simply cannot go on. God steps in.

Second, those who are healed have further work to do for God here below. Sergei's grandmother had a ministry of prayer. The kingdom of God needed her. Sergei told me names of various people, prominent in God's work, who had been brought to the Lord and kept on the "straight and narrow" largely because of her work of intercessory prayer.

Third, God heals and postpones one's death so that His glory may be displayed. Nothing is impossible with God. There comes a time when He chooses to step in and heal miraculously and suddenly to show His power and glory and to put skeptics to silence.

TO THOSE WHO WEEP

When God does not stop our loved ones from dying, He has another way of showing that He cares.

What, then, does He do? He comes to those who weep. Jesus made His way to the exact place where Mary and Martha were. When Martha heard that Jesus was coming, she went out to meet Him. Mary could not bring herself to meet Jesus—she stayed at home. After talking with Jesus for a while, Martha returned to Mary. "The Teacher is here," she said, "and is asking for you" (John 11:28). When Mary saw Jesus, she fell at His feet and said, "Lord, if you had been here, my brother would not have died" (v. 32).

Mary was bitter. Jesus knew that. She wept. Jesus wept. He did not scold her. He did not lecture her. He did not rebuke her. Rather, "Jesus wept" (v. 35), the shortest verse in the Bible.

How does Jesus show that He cares when our loved ones die? He comes and weeps with us. He knows where we are and makes His way there. He knows what we feel and lets us know that He understands. He doesn't show His care by stopping our loved ones from dying, but He shows it by *being there* and weeping with us. Even though Jesus knew God's purpose, He lived in the very present moment with those who *didn't* know what the Lord was going to do.

God lives in the present with us. He knows how things will be tomorrow, and He knows that there will be a better tomorrow. But He lives in the exact present with us because He knows how we feel right now. "The Lord is full of compassion and mercy" (James 5:11).

He Did Not Spare His Own Son

When Jesus was hanging on the cross, there were those who privately said to themselves, "He will never die. Any man who could walk on water, heal the blind, and multiply two fish and five loaves of bread to feed five thousand will not Himself die." But there were also the hostile ones saying, "…save yourself! Come down from the cross, if you are the Son of God!" (Matt. 27:40). And some thought Jesus would do precisely that. After all, if Jesus really was the Son of God, the Father would not allow Him to die. Suddenly Jesus cried out, "'*Eloi, Eloi lama sabachthani'*—which means, 'My God, my God, why have you forsaken me?'" (v. 46).

But Isaiah saw the whole event hundreds of years in advance. He got into the skin of the Jewish people: "…we considered him stricken by God, smitten by him, and afflicted" (Isa. 53:4). This to the Jews was the rationale by which they justified themselves for killing Jesus. They said, "God is doing it. If God is doing it, it shows that Jesus is not really the Son of God."

They were partly right, of course. God was doing it. God was behind it. Jesus *was* smitten of God. Why? Because

"…the LORD has laid on him the iniquity of us all" (v. 6).

God "did not spare his own Son" (Rom. 8:32). We may well keep this in mind when we are tempted to question God for allowing one of our loved ones to die. God did not spare His one and only Son. God could have stopped His Son from dying, but that would have meant that none of us could be saved.

When one of our loved ones is taken from us, it is extremely difficult to see things objectively. But God knows that. This is why He does not shame us or lecture us in our moments of sorrow. Mary would eventually see how wrong she was to accuse Jesus as she did. But she could never forget that Jesus let her get things off her heart. He did not rebuke her once.

God knows how we feel when a loved one is taken from us. Fortunately He does not take us too seriously in our bitterness. "For the wrath of man worketh not the righteousness of God" (James 1:20, KJV). God overlooks our bitterness. That is how much He cares.

By the way, it might be helpful to point out the very scriptures that both my father and I leaned on prior to my mother's death. On the morning he hurried excitedly up the stairs to wake me up, he had just read Psalm 6. His reading that morning made him feel that God knew exactly what he was going through. Psalm 6:6 says, "…All night long I flood my bed with weeping and drench my couch with tears." My dad felt this was a description of himself. He thought Psalm 6:5 meant my mother would not die, and Psalm 6:9 was assurance that she would be healed.

The scripture that gave me so much hope was Psalm

27:14: "Wait on the LORD: be of good courage, and he shall strengthen thine heart: wait, I say, on the LORD" (KJV). I took that to mean that my mother would be healed and not die.

When one examines Psalm 6 and Psalm 27:14 carefully, we can see that there is no definite word that healing would take place. We tend to read into a verse that God gives us and bring more out of it than God intends. If we aren't careful, we can project our wishes on almost any verse rather than let it speak to us as God intends.

When Jesus said the sickness of Lazarus would not end in death but was for the glory of God (John 11:4), we can see how it might be interpreted *before* Lazarus died and *after* Lazarus died. After the whole purpose of God was fulfilled in the lives of Lazarus and his two sisters, one could see that our Lord had said nothing but the truth. God kept His word perfectly.

VINDICATE HIM NOW

There *is* coming a day in which God will clear His name. "God has a lot to answer for," says the unconverted person. "If God is perfectly just and loving, He would not allow famine in Ethiopia, earthquakes in South America, the low standard of living in Calcutta, violence in Northern Ireland, hurricanes in the Gulf states of America, and ruthless men taking advantage of innocent, helpless children."

But God *does* allow evil. God does let man suffer. And He is just and holy and merciful. "The LORD is righteous in all his ways and loving toward all he has made" (Ps. 145:17).

"Rubbish," say the scoffer and the infidel. But God quietly suggests that we lower our voices. "'For my thoughts are not your thoughts, neither are your ways my ways,' declares the LORD. 'As the heavens are higher than the earth, so are my ways higher than your ways and my thoughts than your thoughts'" (Isa. 55:8–9).

The differences between the Christian and the non-Christian can be summed up briefly. The Christian vindicates God now; the non-Christian will vindicate God later. To do so now is to do it willingly and by faith. To do so later is to do it by constraint and without faith. For "faith is being sure of what we hope for and certain of what we do not see" (Heb. 11:1). Secular man says, "Seeing is believing." The Christian says, "Believing is not seeing." We see, yes, but through the eyes of faith. We affirm what God says about Himself in the Word. We vindicate Him *now*—by faith. The non-Christian will vindicate Him later—by sight. For "every eye will see him, even those who pierced him; and all the peoples of the earth will mourn because of him" (Rev. 1:7). Men will call to the mountains and rocks, "Fall on us and hide us from the face of him who sits on the throne and from the wrath of the Lamb! For the great day of their wrath has come, and who can stand?" (Rev. 6:16–17). "'As surely as I live,' says the Lord, 'every knee will bow before me; every tongue will confess to God'" (Rom. 14:11).

The question is, shall we vindicate God now—or later?

3

DOES JESUS CARE WHEN WE ARE AFRAID?

My first memory in the world was when, as a child of two or three years of age, I was left alone one night in the back garden of our home on Central Avenue in Ashland, Kentucky. It seems we had just come back from church. Apparently my father thought I was with my mother. My mother thought I had gone with my father. Neither knew I was left alone at the rear of the garden in the black dark of night. When they heard me screaming they both came out after me. I remember it as though it were yesterday.

All of us have peculiar fears for which there is probably a psychological explanation. They no doubt contribute to the shaping of our personalities, sometimes creating a basis for a neurosis. "Every person is worth understanding," says Christian psychologist Clyde Narramore. If we knew why people behave as they do, we would become more sympathetic.

Fear is one of the most undesirable emotions we have. There are many fears, but here are a few:

- ○ Fear of hunger or thirst

- ○ Fear of being left behind

- ○ Fear of rejection

- ○ Fear of being put to shame

- ○ Fear of an accident

- ○ Fear of illness

- ○ Fear of the outcome of an examination

- ○ Fear of not having sufficient data when making a decision

- ○ Fear of loneliness

- ○ Fear of people

- ○ Fear of suffering

- ○ Fear of death

Josif Tson has pointed out that the phrase "fear not" (or its equivalent) is found 366 times in the Bible—one for every day of the year and an extra one for leap year! God does not want us to be afraid.

Two days after Jesus received the word that His friend Lazarus was unwell, "he said to his disciples, 'Let us go back to Judea'" (John 11:7). His disciples began to panic. "'But Rabbi,' they said, 'a short while ago the Jews tried to stone you, and yet you are going back there?'" (v. 8).

Jesus wasn't afraid, but the disciples were. They tried to mask their fear by acting as though they were looking out for Him. But they knew He wasn't afraid to go back to the same place. He knew why they put it that way.

Sometimes we will not admit to our real feelings. We cover up the way we really feel. This is why we tend to wear a mask all the time. We don't want to let people see us the way we really are. We are equally afraid they won't admire us if they see how human we are.

None of us want to admit to fear. The result is that we repress it instead. Repression is a defense mechanism whereby we deny what we are really feeling. We usually do it involuntarily; that is, we don't even realize what we are doing. Sometimes the thought is so painful that we push the reality down into our unconscious mind, so consciously we only allow ourselves to think about what is not painful. Repression is almost never a good thing. We can push something down into the basement of our being, but it will pop out in the attic in a different form: irritability, high blood pressure, defensiveness, and any number of physical ailments.

AT NIGHT...OR BY DAYLIGHT

It is best to face our fears. Jesus was not going to let His disciples run from danger. "Jesus answered, 'Are there not twelve hours of daylight? A man who walks by day will not stumble, for he sees by this world's light. It is when he walks by night that he stumbles, for he has no light'" (John 11:9–10). There is no great truth in these words as far as I can see. Our Lord was merely saying, "Let's not run from trouble at night."

Nicodemus came to Jesus "at night" (John 3:2). He was a man of considerable prestige—a member of the Sanhedrin (the governing body of the Jews). He was fascinated by Jesus, felt in his heart that Jesus was authentic, and wanted to have an interview with Him. He came at night. In those days, of course, there was no electricity. Thus, unless there was a full moon on a clear night, when night came it was completely dark. People could do things at night that they would not do in the daytime lest they got caught. Jesus said, "...men loved darkness instead of light because their deeds were evil" (John 3:19). This referred, of course, to sin, and evil, as such, sprang from the spiritual kingdom of darkness. But it was also true that more wickedness was committed at night than in broad daylight.

Nicodemus did not want his peers to know he was seeking out Jesus. It was the fear of man that motivated him to have a conversation with Jesus at night. The one thing Jesus was not going to do was run from trouble, not to mention taking advantage of the night in order to be spared. Jesus did not give in to the fear of man. "Are there not twelve hours of daylight?" We will walk in the day!

When Arthur Blessitt reached Nicaragua on his walk from Mexico City to the Darien Jungle, he was warned particularly about the terrorists in Nicaragua. "Whatever you do, don't sleep out in the open at night," numerous people told him.

Arthur replied, "I always sleep where I quit walking."

"Not in Nicaragua you don't," they retorted.

Arthur said, "I've never run up to now. We will sleep where I quit walking during the day." Arthur experienced, on that occasion, one of the most remarkable deliverances from a firing squad that can be imagined in the twentieth century. "After all," explains Arthur, "when you start running, where will you stop?"

Jesus refused to run. "We will walk in the day." To know the background, one must read the latter part of John 10. When Jesus said, "I and the Father are one" (John 10:30), it was too much for the Jews to cope with. "The Jewish leaders picked up stones in order to kill Jesus. But he said, 'I have shown you many good things that my Father sent me to do. Which one are you going to stone me for?' They answered, 'We are not stoning you because of any good thing you did. We are stoning you because you did a terrible thing. You are just a man, and here you are claiming to be God!'" (John 10:31–33, CEV). They tried to seize Him, "but he escaped their grasp" (v. 39).

Jesus knew, again and again, what it was to escape the grasp of hostile men. When He affirmed the sovereignty of God to heal whom He would in the day of Elijah and Elisha, the people of Nazareth became infuriated. They took Him to the brow of the hill on which the town was built in order to throw

Him down the cliff. "But he walked right through the crowd and went on his way" (Luke 4:30). No running; only walking.

When Jesus was finally apprehended, it was because He let it happen. He lived with a perfect faith in His Father and in the Father's purpose. He knew that He would be kept safe until the time came for Him to be arrested.

This did not stop His disciples from being afraid. Although they had watched Jesus escape the grasp of hostile crowds time and time again, they were afraid that their "luck" might run out. Never! says Jesus. We will walk while it is day!

NORMAL AND NEUROTIC FEAR

I would say that there are three kinds of fear: normal fear, neurotic fear, and sinful fear. Normal fear is what I call common sense. When you prepare to cross the street, you look both ways. When you are a Christian, it does not mean that you don't bother to look both ways when you cross the street! Conversion to Christ, no matter how extraordinary it might be, does not take away the instinct of self-preservation. You naturally look both ways when you cross the street. You lock your door when you go out of the house and after you come in.

And yet there is an inherent promise in the gospel that deals with fear. One of the earliest statements with reference to our Lord was that we should be rescued from the hand of our enemies and enabled to serve God "without fear" (Luke 1:74). Paul said to Timothy, "God did not give us a spirit of timidity, but a spirit of power, of love and of self-discipline"

(2 Tim. 1:7). There is therefore a promise, inherent in the gospel, that deals with fear.

Neurotic fear is anxiety without a known cause. There, no doubt, *is* a cause. The cause may be very difficult to trace. It could go back to childhood, even to the womb. We all have neurotic fears by degree. What may be your neurotic fear may not be mine. One person may have a fear of the dark, another person a fear of heights, while another might have a fear of sex, a fear of crowds, a fear of closed places (claustrophobia), a fear of germs, or a fear of cats or dogs. I could go on and on.

Perhaps I have not named your own fear. But carried to an extreme, a fear becomes a sickness. There is a sense that anxiety is the common denominator of all psychopathology. Neurotic fears carried to an extreme become mental illness. All of us are mentally ill to some degree. None of us are absolutely perfect in our emotional and psychological state. Only Jesus was. Fortunately for us, He is *touched* with the *feeling* of our weaknesses. He was tempted at all points as we are but "without sin" (Heb. 4:15).

If I were to disclose some of my own weaknesses, you might say, "I certainly don't have that problem." I don't intend to unveil my weaknesses. The wearing of the mask is wise in some cases. I would do you no favor if I were to spill my heart to you. Nor would you do anyone a favor by doing the same. And yet, the other extreme would be to pretend and falsely convey the impression that we are perfectly balanced in every way. We should be sufficiently transparent not to convey infallibility, making others feel they are the odd ones.

The gospel of Christ does not promise to take away all our neurotic fears. It does not promise to deal *directly* with them. This may come as a disappointment to you. But if you were to turn to Christ merely because you thought all your emotional problems would disappear, you would be seeking Him for the wrong reason. Yes, distress can be God's means to drive you to Himself, but the gospel deals directly with sin and only indirectly with certain fears.

Once the problem of sin is dealt with and we are granted true repentance, there is often a great diminishing of the fears that may have been there for years. Some receive a deliverance almost overnight. Others have to wrestle with the problem. I have known some people to give up certain habits at the moment of conversion, while others (equally converted) had to struggle.

Does Jesus care about our neurotic fears? Yes. Our "great high priest," as He is called (Heb. 4:14), is moved with compassion (Matt. 14:14, KJV). There is no fear that does not concern Him. When the very hairs of our heads are numbered (Matt. 10:30), how much more is our Lord gripped with feeling in the areas where we hurt inside!

HE UNDERSTANDS YOUR FEAR

You may have a problem so terrifying, but it is too sensitive to discuss with another—even your best friend. It is good if you *can* discuss it with another, at least your minister, but never, never, never doubt that our Lord Jesus cares, understands, accepts, loves, and gives strength and guidance. One caution: don't wear the mask with Him. Nothing could be more foolish. He knows all anyway! "All things are naked and opened unto the eyes of him with whom we have to do" (Heb. 4:13, KJV). Our heavenly Father knows what you need even before you ask Him (Matt. 6:8). Don't play the game with God. Unburden your heart to Him. Tell Him *everything*. Hide absolutely nothing. You will find that He does not scold, laugh, moralize, or rebuke. He is touched. Hallelujah, what a God!

Are you afraid? Jesus understands. He knew that His disciples were worried about themselves, not Him. But He let them know straightaway that He would not let them run from the problem. He made them face it. Do not be surprised if our Lord will not allow you to run from your problem. He accepts us as we are—not because He approves, but because He knows we need Him and all the help He can give us.

But we must be willing to let Him help us. We must walk in the day. We must not hide at night or run from the problem by retreating to darkness. In many years of being a pastor, I have learned this: Most people don't want their problems solved. They want them understood. The thing is, I might understand your problem; I might not. But in any case, I cannot help those who do not want help.

Jesus accepts us so that He might teach us repentance. We must come openly before Him and be utterly willing to walk in the light He gives. God does not lead us directly from A to Z, but from A to B, B to C, etc. Ask God to lead you to B.

The marvel is, He *does* understand. Many people come to me with problems I don't understand. Why? Because I haven't had the same problems. I may look at them and do my very best to sympathize and understand, but I have not been "tempted in every way" (Heb. 4:15). It is marvelous when I *can* relate to a person's problem. It makes them feel better and certainly know they are at least understood—and not odd! We like to think the other person who offers sympathy really *does* sympathize.

On the evening before my mother's funeral, friends of my father and myself came to the funeral home to pay their respects. My father was seated in a room, in a corner, usually not bothering to even stand as friends walked by to say, "We are sorry. We extend our sincerest sympathy." My father said, "Thank you, thank you." Suddenly I noticed that he stood up. He looked toward the door of the room as a man walked in to see him. My father said, "Here's a man who can sympathize with me." They fell into each other's arms and sobbed openly. Most people there understood. The other man had lost his wife a few weeks before.

But our Lord is one who understands and sympathizes with *every* problem. I can sympathize with one who has lost a mother or who may have had a traumatic experience in the dark as a child. There are certainly many other areas in which I can sympathize with those who have needs. But with Jesus, we have One who is totally sympathetic with every problem— tempted in *every* way that we are.

THEN THERE IS SINFUL FEAR

What about sinful fear? It is what springs from "sinful nature" (Eph. 2:3) and is at least three things: fear of man, fear of insecurity, and fear of death. Does the gospel deal with these in a direct manner? Yes, because the gospel deals directly with sin. The fears we have by "nature" are owing to sin. By nature, then, I mean sinful man. The fear of man is due to sin—nothing else.

The fear of man is a motivation to please man, not God. Jesus asked, "How can you believe if you accept praise from one another, yet make no effort to obtain the praise that comes from the only God?" (John 5:44). Peer pressure is nothing but the fear of man. It is looking over our shoulders to see what "they" will think—will they approve or disapprove? It shows we are captive to others. We are anything but our own when we are governed by the approval of others.

This is why we are commanded to come out of hiding when we become Christians. "Whoever acknowledges me before men, I will also acknowledge him before my Father in heaven" (Matt. 10:32). Paul said, "If you confess with your mouth, 'Jesus is Lord,' and believe in your heart that God raised him from the dead, you will be saved" (Rom. 10:9). There must be this twofold operation: heart belief and open confession. Why? This shows that you are beginning to make headway with reference to the fear of man. Thus the first thing you are commanded to do as a Christian is to show that you are unashamed!

"The LORD is my light and my salvation—whom shall I fear? The LORD is the stronghold of my life—of whom shall I be afraid?" (Ps. 27:1). Peter asked, "Who is going to harm you if you are eager to do good?" (1 Pet. 3:13).

The gospel does not deal with normal fear and only indirectly with neurotic fear, but it meets head-on the fear that springs from our rebellion, our sinfulness, against God.

HE WILL MEET ALL YOUR NEEDS

The fear of insecurity is dealt with by our walking in the light (1 John 1:7). In the Sermon on the Mount, Jesus upbraided men for the fear of want. It was a command that you should "not worry about your life, what you will eat or drink; or about your body, what you will wear" (Matt. 6:25). Paul said that the "love of money is a root of all kinds of evil" (1 Tim. 6:10). Many of us like to think we are exempt from the love of money merely because we do not expect (or want) to live in luxury. But the fear of whether or not our needs will be supplied springs from the same bitter well.

The task of the Christian is to walk in the light and develop faith to the degree that our obedience to Christ is *never* in jeopardy of owing to financial considerations. When God tells us to "go" we must *move*. Once we begin to lag behind due to fear of how our need will be supplied, the devil will slip in, and, before we know it, we shall have completely rationalized away God's call.

The fear of insecurity needs to be dealt with in a radical manner. "And my God will meet *all your needs* according to his glorious riches in Christ Jesus" (Phil. 4:19, emphasis added). My father's favorite verse was: "But seek first his kingdom and his righteousness, and all these things will be given to you as well" (Matt. 6:33). As long as Satan can succeed in tempting us to worry about financial and material things, our discipleship will never rise above second class. "No one who puts his hand to the plow and looks back is fit for service in the kingdom of God" (Luke 9:62).

We must walk in the day. No fear of man. No fear of insecurity. There must be a trust that the same God who supplied the need in the past will do it again. Our Lord was delivered from the hostility of men time and time again; why start now by walking at night?

> Through many dangers, toils and snares,
> I have already come;
> 'Tis grace hath brought me safe thus far,
> And grace will lead me home.[1]
>
> —JOHN NEWTON

DEATH: A "NATURAL" FEAR

The fear of death is a natural fear. By "natural" I do not mean merely normal. I mean the fear that has its origin in sin. Jesus shared in our humanity "...so that by his death he might destroy him who holds the power of death—that is, the devil—and free those who all their lives were held in slavery by their fear of death" (Heb. 2:14–15). This verse suggests that all fear is ultimately traceable to the fear of death. Take away the fear of death and you have a free man. Josif Tson once said to me, "The most dangerous man in the world is the one who is not afraid to die."

The gospel gives assurance of heaven. The gospel is concerned about your death. I have a little tract called *What*

Is Christianity? We have given them out by the tens of thousands. When we first sent the manuscript to a Christian printer, it was sent back by this printer who thought he was so clever. "Tell Dr. Kendall he's got it wrong. Surely this tract should read that Christianity is essentially concerned about your life." We gave it to a different printer. I knew exactly what I wanted to say in the pamphlet: "Christianity is essentially concerned about your death."

On the first Saturday in 1986, I had a most unusual experience. As we were getting ready for another morning of witnessing on the streets of London, I began to feel that this was one Saturday I didn't want to have to face the people and the cold—it was bitterly cold. As I walked out of Westminster Chapel yard toward Buckingham Gate, an awful depression came on me. I had never known anything like it in my four years of Pilot Light work. I began to feel that our being out on the streets was useless. "What have I done?" I asked myself. "I told all these people to leave their homes, and here I go myself. Is it really worth it?"

I can tell you that in no fewer than fifteen seconds a total stranger walked up to me and asked, "Are you Dr. Kendall?"

"Yes," I answered.

"Are you the Dr. Kendall who wrote this tract?" he further asked, showing me my *What Is Christianity?* tract.

"I'm the one," I replied.

"Would you talk with me for a few minutes?" he continued.

"Sure," I said. "What's the problem?"

"Last week," he stated, "one of your people gave me this

little pamphlet. I am a taxi driver. I must have had a thousand things given to me like this in the last thirty years, but for some reason I didn't throw this one away. When I came to that part 'Christianity is essentially concerned about your death,' it shook me rigid. Nothing has ever troubled me so much in all my life. I drove to this place this morning to find your address. I was going to write to you. They told me you were here. I didn't expect to meet you." We sat in the back of his taxi on that cold morning, and within an hour I led him to Christ. It was like tapping a ripe plum that fell into my hand.

Martin Luther called John 3:16 "the Bible in a nutshell": "For God so loved the world, that he gave his only begotten Son, that whosoever believeth in him should not perish, but have everlasting life" (KJV). The assumption of Jesus in those lines was that *all men are perishing*. That is why Jesus died. This is why John the Baptist warned, "Flee from the coming wrath" (Matt. 3:7). "Just as man is destined to die once, and after that to face judgment" (Heb. 9:27), so man is going to have to spend eternity somewhere. It is either heaven or hell.

Face Your Fear in the Daylight

There is no greater peace than *knowing* that when you die, you will wake up in heaven with Jesus. You can know this!

Does Jesus care when we are afraid? Yes, He cares. But He makes us face fear in the daylight and enables us to do it.

There's an old axiom about a person who fell from a horse. Whereas one's instinct is that he will never get on a horse again, the best thing he can do is to get right back on and ride it. I think this idea is partly implied in our story about Jesus and His disciples having to go back to Judea in the daylight. They barely escaped being stoned. But the only way for them to conquer their fear was to go right back.

We can overcome the fear of man by confessing Christ and witnessing for Him—anywhere.

We can overcome the fear of insecurity by seeking His glory first and then trusting Him to supply every need. He will do it!

We can overcome the fear of death by acknowledging our sinfulness and Christ's deity and right to rule us, pleading nothing but the blood that He shed on the cross, repenting of our sins, and giving Him our lives. Great peace will follow when you do this from your very heart.

This is why Jesus came. We, then, serve Him "without fear" (Luke 1:74). We aren't ready to live until we are ready to die. When we are ready to die, we begin to explore a whole new world. Everything will look different. People will seem to have changed. Why? Because you have changed! What is more, we can begin to live with ourselves—to be at peace with ourselves. Even the neurotic fears take on a new perspective, if only because our Lord Jesus Christ understands them and doesn't accept us on the basis of our worthiness.

By the way, Nicodemus eventually came out of hiding. He did a most courageous thing in the end. After having been a "secret" disciple for a little while, Nicodemus confessed Christ at a time when it took more courage than most men can muster in a lifetime. He joined Joseph of Arimathea, a fellow member of the Sanhedrin and also a "secret" disciple, and openly took Jesus's body down from the cross and anointed it (John 19:40). They did this before Pilate the governor, as well as crowds of people who watched Jesus die. What courage! What a confession!

What made Nicodemus do it? He did it at a time, humanly speaking, that could not have been worse. Jesus was now dead. What good would it do now to confess to be His follower? Answer: Nicodemus believed that Jesus would be raised from the dead. He wanted to get in his confession while there was still room for faith. Remember, faith is believing without seeing the evidence. Had Nicodemus waited until Jesus was raised, it would have been, by comparison, a lesser confession.

Perhaps Nicodemus was ashamed that he spent months in hiding. But when Jesus was dying on the cross, Nicodemus vowed to do something about coming out in the open for Him—in the daylight—while there was still time to look like an utter fool in the eyes of men.

Does Jesus care when we are afraid? Yes. He understands. By accepting us as we are, He can make us what He is—a man of faith, a man of courage. God wants to do that for you.

4

DOES JESUS CARE WHEN WE MISUNDERSTAND HIM?

I shall never forget hearing a sermon on the radio one morning. I'm sure the preacher loves the Lord as much as I do, if not more, but he was dealing with a particular verse in the Bible that he clearly did not understand. He was out of his depth. He went on and on. The more he preached, the more painful it was. It became agony to listen, and in the end, I turned to another station.

My thought at the time was, "Lord, why do You allow such nonsense to go out under Your name?" I asked Him, "Lord, Your name is at stake. Don't You care?" Now, there are times when a particular verse may be open to more than one valid interpretation. But in this case the man was quite wrong and, so it seemed to me, could only do harm to the cause of Christ. Why did God allow this? Why doesn't God stop those who perpetrate error in His name? What confusion people will have! "Why, Lord, do You allow this?"

That was many, many years ago. I still think that preacher was wrong, but events over the last several decades have given me pause. I have reassessed certain things I once believed. I too have changed what I believed with regard to certain texts. I too was preaching over the radio to thousands every Sunday morning back in 1966. I now say a number of things differently. God didn't stop *me* then. He allowed me to go on, even though I misunderstood Him—that is, His Word.

God is so gracious to us. All of us naturally want to assume that—now—we have it right. Perhaps we didn't have it right yesterday or a few years ago, but now we are ready and able. But are we? I am sobered at the thought that I have a lot of changing to do, even theologically and in my understanding of certain verses. Perhaps I *don't* need a lot of theological surgery performed on my heart and mind. Perhaps I do. I should be very surprised indeed to find that I am totally free from error in my treatment of every verse.

But God still uses me. I may blush tomorrow when I have to take back certain things I have said today. And yet, I hope I shall have the courage and integrity to admit it when I need to change. I have painfully observed those who would not be open to an alternative position if they already had gone "on record" for a particular interpretation. It is amazing how much sheer pride can influence our treatment of certain verses in the Bible.

Yes, I was horrified at what that radio preacher said so many years ago. But no doubt God was using him. I trust that God continues to use me, even if I have a lot of defects. Paul said—a verse of no small comfort to any minister— "But we have this treasure in jars of clay to show that this all-surpassing power is from God and not from us" (2 Cor. 4:7). God overrules our weaknesses, even risking our failure to represent His holy name very well.

He Made Himself Vulnerable

There is to be seen in this chapter one of the strangest, most surprising, and yet quite obvious characteristics about God: He has willingly made Himself vulnerable. God Almighty, the Most High God, has made Himself vulnerable. *Vulnerable* simply means "the capacity to be wounded or hurt; liable to injury; like a lamb." A lamb is so vulnerable. A child is so vulnerable. God has made Himself vulnerable.

Now, this is an aspect of God's nature that many people don't see—or don't want to see. Some of us are threatened by the possibility that God has made Himself vulnerable. It seems incongruous or unsuitable to us that God could be omnipotent (all powerful), omniscient (all wise), and omnipresent (present everywhere) and still be vulnerable in a very real sense. But it is true.

The two most important things the Bible says about God are that He is merciful and just. If I had to summarize God to the non-Christian, it would be in that manner. God's mercy means He does not want to punish you. But His justice means He *must* punish you—because you are a sinner. The most important and crucial question of all is, how can God be just and merciful at the same time?

And yet I want to say the characteristic that is most unusual is God's vulnerability to being misunderstood. It shows how great God is and how *big* God is.

Most of us work overtime to keep from being misunderstood. If I hear that you have misunderstood me, it may almost drive me crazy until I sit down with you and clarify things. Are you not much the same? If you hear that someone said something about you that is not true, don't you want to set the record straight?

Now why is it that we work overtime to correct being misunderstood? Why are we so anxious to set the record straight? It is because our self-esteem is at stake. We care what others think about us because our self-esteem is threatened.

Now think about this. We are talking about the Most High God—the God of glory and power who said, "I am the LORD; that is my name! I will not give my glory to another or my praise to idols" (Isa. 42:8). And yet, God has made Himself vulnerable by allowing Himself to be misunderstood.

But in doing so, He simultaneously lets us think He doesn't care. By becoming "weak" (1 Cor. 1:25), He puts His reputation on the line by which men will conclude: the God up there doesn't care.

How can God be like this? Why is He like this? How could God make Himself vulnerable in this manner? The answer to these questions is really very simple: He is secure in Himself. There is no insecurity in God.

SOME MIGHT MISUNDERSTAND

The reason we are so anxious to clarify misunderstandings about ourselves is that we are so insecure. We can't bear to think we have been misunderstood. If people want to reject us because they *have* understood us, fine. But when their rejection is traceable to misunderstandings of who or what we are and have said, the consequence is painful and frustrating.

But God is not like that. He is not insecure in Himself. God is free. It is our bondage that forces us to defend ourselves. Freedom is being at peace with ourselves—*we* know what we did and said—*others* not understanding us have the problem. This is not to say that we should not seek to be clear. But there is a point at which we must rest our case with a good conscience. God has a good conscience. The highest level of freedom is having nothing to prove. Otherwise we may fall into the "protest too much" syndrome, as Shakespeare said: "Methinks thou dost protest too much." Overstating betrays insecurity in ourselves.

Jesus let Himself be misunderstood by Mary and Martha. He even let His own disciples misunderstand Him by staying in the same place for two more days rather than going to Lazarus straightaway. He did not bother to explain to them why He stayed put two more days.

What is more, after walking in the direction of Bethany, the home of Lazarus, Jesus said, "'Our friend Lazarus has fallen asleep; but I am going there to wake him up.' His disciples replied, 'Lord, if he sleeps, he will get better'" (John 11:11–12). They misunderstood His language. Why He used language like that, knowing they would interpret it as they did, I don't know. Perhaps Jesus wanted to get us to reinterpret how we see saved people who die—they sleep. Paul referred to the "dead in Christ" as being those who had "fallen asleep" (1 Thess. 4:15–16). Jesus then told His disciples plainly, "Lazarus is dead" (John 11:14). This shows that God can, when He chooses, step in and clarify things. When He does, it is because it's what we need at the time. When He doesn't, it is because we can cope for the time being.

There was one occasion when Jesus used the word *sleep* to describe a dead person. When a local ruler asked Jesus to raise his daughter from the dead, Jesus agreed to do it. When Jesus entered the ruler's house and saw the flute players and the noisy crowd, He said that the girl was but asleep. "And they laughed him to scorn" (Matt. 9:24, KJV). Jesus calmly ordered the crowd to be put outside. He went in, took the girl by the hand, "and the maid arose" (v. 25, KJV).

When God recognizes that people misunderstand Him, He does not panic. He knows that it is merely a matter of time until all will know what He is about and why He permits what He does. That is not to say He is not grieved and that He does not feel the hurt. It is that He is too great and too big to stoop to answer the crowds.

And Jesus plainly stated that Lazarus was dead.

SULKING THOMAS

Thomas, one of the Twelve, said, "Let us also go, that we may die with him" (John 11:16). Thomas is often referred to as "doubting Thomas" because of his famous statement about

Jesus's appearance to ten of the other disciples after His resurrection, "Unless I see the nail marks in his hands and put my finger where the nails were, and put my hand into his side, I will not believe it" (John 20:25). I prefer to speak of him as "sulking Thomas." I have thought that Thomas was sulking as much as he was doubting. He surely knew in his heart that the ten disciples would not have made up the story about seeing Jesus. And yet Jesus took him at face value and later said to Thomas, "Put your finger here; see my hands. Reach out your hand and put it into my side. Stop doubting and believe" (v. 27). Our Lord has an extraordinary way of letting us save face.

There is some dispute among Bible commentators as to the meaning of Thomas's statement in John 11:16: "Let us also go, that we may die with him." Who is the "him"? Was it Jesus who, should He be stoned in Judea, would be killed; hence Thomas was speaking somewhat heroically about dying with Jesus? Or was "him" referring to Lazarus, since Jesus had just said that Lazarus was dead? I take the latter view. I think that Thomas said, "Let us also go, that we may die with Lazarus."

But why would Thomas make a statement like that? I think he was sulking. He knew that Mary and Martha had sent for Jesus. Thomas may have said to himself, "If this is love, then why does He let Lazarus die?" It seems to me that Thomas was virtually saying, "The Lord let Lazarus die, and He will let us die too." This is why Thomas said, "Let us *also* go, that we may die with him" (John 11:16, emphasis added). I think that Thomas wanted to get a response from Jesus. He was "baiting" Him, to see exactly what Jesus would say.

In any case, Thomas misunderstood Jesus. Jesus might have explained His purpose to Thomas on the spot. After all, Thomas was one of the Twelve. Surely Jesus could have shared with the Twelve what He was going to do, but not one of the Twelve knew what Jesus was planning.

No Private Interpretations

Our Lord does not always share His *own* interpretation of His Word to us. He may give us a word without giving the absolute interpretation. "No prophecy of the scripture is of any private interpretation" (2 Pet. 1:20, KJV). But there are times when we feel barren of the *true* interpretation and we have to settle for a "private" one. Sometimes He gives us the correct one after we have preached or written for years on a subject or verse, at long last showing us the real meaning. It happens often.

Why? I don't know. Perhaps it is to keep us humble in the meantime, lest we fancy ourselves to be the only infallible interpreters of Scripture. In any case, God allows us to misunderstand Him, to continue with certain plans that may not be right, and to interpret His Word in a way that may not be correct. Wonder of wonders, He uses it anyway!

Our Lord in heaven does not dispatch an angel to correct us every time we err with His Word. He is not so worried about His reputation in the world that He listens to us and says, "Oh no! I can't let R. T. Kendall perpetrate a view like that. What will people think of Me now?" No. He uses earthen vessels and has the patience to wait for the day when

He will put the record straight. What a day of blushing that will be!

God even allows men to go into the ministry without education or preparation. I was in the ministry for years before I went to seminary. He uses men who are ill prepared, filled with self-pity, ambitious, jealous, insecure, proud, and even vindictive. "For he knoweth our frame; he remembereth that we are dust" (Ps. 103:14, kjv). In 1984, the Reverend Jesse Jackson ran for president of the United States. Along the way, he brought the house down at the Democratic National Convention when he seemed to plead for their patience and said, "God isn't finished with me yet!"

God wasn't finished with Thomas. But what did Jesus say in response to Thomas? Nothing. Not a word. That is often the way the Lord reacts to us when we make thoughtless comments. He kindly ignores us. We may think we can manipulate God into reacting to us, but "the wrath of man worketh not the righteousness of God" (James 1:20, kjv). Sometimes God puts us in our place best by His silence.

Perhaps you thought you would get God's attention by shaking your fist at Him. Perhaps you thought He would be so provoked by your blasphemy that He would come to you in thunder and lightning.

Many years ago, a rather flamboyant atheist came to speak in a large auditorium in Ashland, Kentucky. He claimed to have the ultimate proof that God does not exist. After giving his lecture, he closed it with a proposition he made with God—on the spot—"If God exists, let Him strike me dead within fifteen minutes." In the meantime he cursed

God, blasphemed, and did everything imaginable in order to make God angry enough to strike the man down in front of everyone.

He took out his pocket watch, set it on the lectern and waited for God to strike him dead. People watched in a hushed silence. As the seconds ticked away and came to the fifteen-minute mark, tension filled the auditorium. Then the man made his pronouncement, "See there, folks. There is no God." But while the auditorium was still deathly quiet and tense, a young boy shouted from the rear of the auditorium, "Sir, do you think that you can exhaust the patience of God in fifteen minutes?"

Some people may think that God is obliged to speak to us in our moment of urgent need. If He seems not to, this, to my mind, excuses them for their unbelief. It is man's subtle way of saying to God, "If You really want me to believe in You, then You must behave in a more respectable way."

BY PREACHING JESUS

Jesus said, "A wicked and adulterous generation looks for a miraculous sign, but none will be given it except the sign of Jonah" (Matt. 16:4). And what was the sign of Jonah? Preaching. Jonah marched into Nineveh with a simple but direct message, "Forty more days and Nineveh will be overturned" (Jon. 3:4). Paul said, "For since in the wisdom of God the world through its wisdom did not know him, God was pleased through the foolishness of what was preached to save those who believe" (1 Cor. 1:21).

In other words, God convinces men of Himself by preaching Jesus Christ. When Paul came to Corinth—the seat of learning and sensuality of the day—where there was no "God framework," he said, "For I resolved to know nothing while I was with you except Jesus Christ and him crucified" (1 Cor. 2:2). Paul, knowing that he was going to the famous Corinth, might have said to himself, "I'd better bone up on my Aristotle and Plato if I am going to a place like Corinth. I must show myself to be the erudite man they will listen to."

But no. He knew there was only *one way* men would be convinced of the true God, and that was by preaching Jesus Christ. As Peter put it, "Through him you believe in God" (1 Pet. 1:21).

We can't possibly know everything—it is not all explained to us. Above all, if we know that we are saved—born again and prepared for heaven when we die—all else becomes unimportant by comparison. Take eschatology (the doctrine that deals with "last things"), for example. How things will turn out in the end is of immense interest to us, but no one knows for sure (that I know of) how the details of the Book of Revelation are to be understood. No two books written on the subject agree entirely on the finer points. This tells me that God must not consider this of crucial importance to us.

When I first went to London and Westminster Chapel, I remember someone asking me if I was a premillennialist (the belief that Jesus will come *before* the one-thousand-year reign of Christ as it is described in Revelation 20), a postmillennialist (the belief that Jesus will come *after* the millennium), or an amillennialist (the belief that the one thousand years

mentioned in Revelation 20 are to be interpreted symboli-
cally). I said, "I've been right *once*." For I do believe that I have
embraced each of these views at some period in my life. If
only I knew when I got it right. I then concluded that I am a
pan-millennialist, because I believe everything will *pan* out
all right in the end.

And yet God uses men, whatever their millennial views
seem to be—even those who make their own particular view
or point of orthodoxy. I wonder what God in heaven thinks
when He sees us so exercised below on certain matters.

SO THAT YOU MAY BELIEVE

When Jesus told His disciples plainly, "Lazarus is dead," He
went on to say what I think may well be the most profound
statement in the entire story: "And for your sake I am glad I
was not there, *so that you may believe*" (John 11:15, emphasis
added). This sentence is the key to faith. Remember, faith is
being sure of what we hope for and certain of what we do
not *see* (Heb. 11:1). Faith is believing something with all your
heart but not having the tangible evidence to prove it to
another person.

Therefore, when Jesus uttered the phrase "so that you may
believe," He showed that faith is what one is privileged to
exercise *in advance* of the undoubted evidence of His perfect
plan. He let them know that they should trust His wisdom
in allowing Lazarus to die without their needing to have a
spoon-fed explanation first. "Trust me," Jesus was virtually
saying to them. "I know that you don't understand why I did

not go and heal My friend Lazarus. Yes, I did let him die. He is dead. But I am glad for your sakes that I did not go and heal him, so that you may trust Me and believe now that I know what I am doing. You will see this clearly later. Trust this to be absolutely true now."

To put it another way, Jesus could not have made this statement, "so that you may believe," at the end of John 11:15. By then they would indeed affirm His wisdom and power and purpose. After the whole reason for Jesus not healing Lazarus was unveiled, anyone could say, "I do believe in Your wisdom and purpose now." But even though we might use the word *believe*, it is not true faith.

Those who were scoffing at Jesus when He was dying on the cross said, "...come down now from the cross, that we may *see and believe*" (Mark 15:32, emphasis added). "See and believe" is the order that the unbeliever always demands. Proof first, faith later, says the atheist. But it isn't faith if the proof precedes.

But someone will say, "Surely this is irrational. How can God expect intelligent people to believe without evidence?" Because God has *chosen* to make Himself known *by faith alone*.

Yes, God *could* have done it another way. God could have let wisdom, for example, be the link that connects us to Himself. According to Paul, God actually thought of that: "In the wisdom of God the world by wisdom knew not God" (1 Cor. 1:21, KJV). In other words, God considered making "wisdom" the way by which men see who He is. But in His own wisdom, He rejected that option. There may be a thousand other options God passed by for all I know. What I do know is that "God was pleased through the foolishness of what was preached to save those *who believe*" (1 Cor. 1:21, emphasis added).

God decreed that the righteous shall live "by faith" (Rom. 1:17). We may not like His choice of how to make Himself known to mankind, but that is the way He did it. It is a most wonderful thing, therefore, when God gives us opportunity to believe. It is a marvelous thing indeed. For once we have the tangible evidence that we may claim what we wish for, faith will no longer be a possibility. And since God has decreed that men only know Him by faith, the worst thing that can happen to a person is to get his wish fulfilled and be given the "evidence" for God instead.

For God *will* give the evidence of Himself one day: "Look, he is coming with the clouds, and every eye will see him, even those who pierced him; and all the peoples of the earth will mourn because of him. So shall it be! Amen" (Rev. 1:7). People will weep, wail, and gnash their teeth at the sight. Maybe they will even say, "I believe now." But it will not be saving faith at work. Rather it will be that they *look* on Jesus, whom they denied when His Word was presented to them.

Thus, when Jesus said to His disciples, "I am glad I was not there, so that you may believe" (John 11:15), He was presenting them an opportunity to *trust Him*—His secret purpose—on a silver platter.

You Can Trust It

There is only one way that you can please God: by faith. "And without faith it is impossible to please God, because anyone who comes to him must believe that he exists and that he rewards those who earnestly seek him" (Heb. 11:6).

"But how *can* I believe that God exists?" you ask. I answer: can you not begin by agreeing with Him on what you *know* is true? Consider what God has said about *you*. You know that you are a sinner, don't you? Only God has told you that. No other source in this whole world would come up with "God talk" like that. Sin. This three-letter word would not be known were it not for the God of the Bible. It is "missing the mark." (That is what *hamartia*, the Greek word for "sin," means.) It is falling short of God's "glory" (Rom. 3:23). It is "lawlessness" (1 John 3:4). It is knowing what you ought to do and not doing it (James 4:17).

Where in the world will you get the best explanation of man's condition but in the Bible? Despite our advancements in technology, learning, expertise, culture, and wonderful achievements, is not man the same as ever? Why is it that politicians can be brilliant in Congress or the Senate but unable to keep their homes together? Why is it that doctors can be brilliant in surgery but a failure as a wife or husband? Why is it that scientists can be brilliant in the laboratory but still be prone to jealousy, greed, pride, lust, and all those things that keep them as unhappy and frustrated people? Why? Answer: sin.

Only the Bible explains man's plight. Only the Bible explains how mankind can be helped. It is by God sending His one and only Son into this world to die on the cross. Why did Jesus die? "For our sins" (1 Cor. 15:3).

When the mobs were shouting to Jesus, "Come down now

from the cross, that we may see and believe," Jesus in fact *stayed right there on that cross so they could believe.* Jesus might have answered those who were shouting at Him with these words, "I am glad for your sake that I am not coming down so that you may believe." The reason He was there was to atone for our sins.

The only way we can be saved is to trust God's integrity—the integrity of His Word, His purpose, and His gospel. By the way, you *can* trust it! You will never be deceived. You will never be let down. "Anyone who trusts in him will never be put to shame" (Rom. 10:11). He promised, "Never will I leave you; never will I forsake you" (Heb. 13:5).

I myself have found this to be true. I know that God is real. He is real to me. He loves me. He cares for me. He hides His face from me, yes. He does it unexpectedly too. But He knows how much I can bear. "No temptation has seized you except what is common to man. And God is faithful; he will not let you be tempted [or tried] beyond what you can bear. But when you are tempted [or tried], he will also provide a way out so that you can stand up under it" (1 Cor. 10:13). As the psalmist put it, "Weeping may remain for a night, but rejoicing comes in the morning" (Ps. 30:5).

God lets us misunderstand His work. The greatest work He ever did was accomplished by His Son Jesus Christ on the cross. But who understood it at the time? There is that old African American spiritual that says, "Were you there when they crucified my Lord?"[1] I can tell you, had you been physically present at the scene of the Crucifixion, you would not have seen a thing, as far as the chief thing that was being accomplished was concerned. To the naked eye it was only another Roman crucifixion (they had them all the time in those days). The curious thing about Jesus's crucifixion was that He was the same person who had done so many wonderful things and whose "sin" was that He admitted to being the King of the Jews (Luke 23:3). But Jesus was not the sort of king they wanted, so they rejected Him.

God Has a Strategy

After Jesus was raised from the dead, Peter proclaimed, "Therefore let all Israel be assured of this: God has made this Jesus, whom you crucified, both Lord and Christ" (Acts 2:36). Jesus is at this very moment at the right hand of God. He *reigns* there. He is King. "For he must reign until he has put all his enemies under his feet" (1 Cor. 15:25).

But this work of God was misunderstood. It was only by the coming of the Holy Spirit on the disciples at Pentecost that all things fell into place for them. They had not known why Jesus died. Even when He was raised from the dead, they did not know why He died or why He was raised. It was only when the Holy Spirit fell on the Day of Pentecost that everything cohered. They all saw it! His death on the cross was God's way of saving man. Our sins were punished in Jesus. He bore them *as though* He were the guilty one. As Isaiah put it, "The LORD has laid on him the iniquity of us all" (Isa. 53:6).

But until the Holy Spirit came, God allowed Himself to be misunderstood. Does He care? Yes. So much that He *asks* us to believe. "I am glad that I did not do what was wanted at first so that you may believe."

God lets us misunderstand His ways. God has a strategy of His own. Our Lord knew exactly what He was going to do. God had a perfect strategy.

God has a will for you—a perfect will. You will never know what it is until you trust Him. You must commit your life wholly to Him. St. Augustine said it best a long time ago, "Thou hast made us for Thyself...and our hearts are restless until they find their rest in Thee."[2]

God lets us misunderstand His secrecy. God can keep a secret. The best-kept secret from the foundation of the world was God's design in sending His Son to the cross. When Jesus died on the cross, Satan thought he had scored the most ingenious victory and pulled the most brilliant coup that ever was. Wrong! God was behind the whole thing. Paul said, "None of the rulers of this age understood it, for if they had, they would not have crucified the Lord of glory" (1 Cor. 2:8).

God lets us misunderstand His sensitivity. Jesus did not let the disciples know what He was really feeling at the time. But He gave a hint: "For your sake I am glad I was not there, so that you may believe" (John 11:15). This lets us know how deeply our Lord felt and how much He wanted them to trust Him totally.

When Thomas made his impertinent comment, Jesus said nothing. Jesus was being just like the Holy Spirit when He is grieved. Quiet. The Holy Spirit can be grieved (Eph. 4:30). The most sensitive person who ever was is the Holy Spirit. When the Holy Spirit is grieved, He does not say so. He just quietly, silently, unobtrusively withdraws. You don't realize it until later. A man by the name of Samson grieved the Lord by betraying the secret of his great power to a temptress whose name was Delilah. The Bible says that Samson "...did not know that the LORD had left him" (Judg. 16:20). But he soon found out.

When you grieve the Holy Spirit, no lights flash, no thunder roars. This is why we must take His Word seriously when it is offered to us. "I tell you, now is the time of God's favor, now is the day of salvation" (2 Cor. 6:2).

God lets us misunderstand His slowness. All of us may wish at first that God would act sooner than He does. I have a prayer list of nearly one hundred items for which I have been praying daily for a long time. I don't know why God is so slow in meeting my requests, but He has a reason. Of that I am absolutely sure. How do I know? By His Word and by experience. His Word tells me that He has a plan and will of His own. My own experience has taught me that God is never too late, never too early, but always just on time!

Any disappointment we may have is God's hint that He has a better idea in mind—if we will but wait.

I know this too. When the disciples saw what Jesus's strategy was in the end, they were not disappointed. Neither will you be. Just remember that He cares so much that He is gently teaching you to trust Him—now.

5

DOES JESUS CARE WHEN WE BLAME HIM?

Arthur Blessitt told me of something that happened to him when he was carrying his cross in Italy. He was prepared to spend the night on a bench. He had no raincoat, only the clothes on his back. It was cold—very cold—snowy, and rainy. He was exhausted from the day's walk and looked forward to a good night's rest. So he looked at the rain and said, "Lord, in the name of Jesus, stop the rain." No sooner had he uttered those words than a loud crash of thunder was heard and the rain began to pour twice as hard, beating against his face and body. Arthur then looked up at the sky and said, "God, I love You anyway. It will take more than water to drown my love for You."

Most of us are not like that. We are more like Mary and Martha who blamed Jesus for their brother's death.

There is something in all of us that instinctively wants to blame God for everything we don't like. One does not need a degree from Harvard to know how to accuse God; no course is needed; no examination required. All of us get this by nature: the feeling that God owes us something and that He is to blame for the troubles of the world.

Some time ago, when we lived in England, my wife, Louise, worked on a Saturday as a Pilot Light—a team of people who go out into the streets and witness and share about Jesus—just a few yards from Victoria station. A very strange man came to her there and began to utter unimaginable things about Jesus Christ—we are convinced he was a classic case of demon possession. It was a traumatic experience for Louise, leaving her in a very fragile state for hours. She had never run across anyone like that. She kept saying, "Why did God let that happen to me?" I replied that I certainly did not know, but I was so glad that it hadn't happened to her on her first day on the streets.

We all have these thoughts when trouble comes, especially when we have prayed in advance.

WHY, LORD?

There are, in fact, two statements that will bear our examination. The first was by both Martha and Mary, "Lord…if you had been here, my brother would not have died" (John 11:21). The second: "Could not he who opened the eyes of the blind man have kept this man from dying?" (v. 37).

The first statement was made by believers—two women who believed in Jesus and were devoted to Him. The second statement was made by unbelievers—those who really hated Jesus.

At first glance, the two statements appear to be alike. But there is a difference between the two. In fact, the difference is so crucial that it provides an index by which you may know whether you are a Christian. Discovering the difference between the two statements will show you.

The first statement was made by Martha, then repeated by Mary. That two women who believed in Jesus's authority and power (as they did) could also make such an unguarded but honest comment is a consoling reminder that Christians can express bitterness.

We all need to be reminded from time to time that even a Christian can be discouraged. Sometimes a Christian can utter a statement that parallels the sentiment of the non-Christian. Even an undoubting Christian can have thoughts of bewilderment, abandonment, and dismay. "Why, God? Why did You allow it?"

Now both of these statements have in common the element of wanting to blame God—but with an important difference.

LORD, IF YOU HAD...

Let us look first at the statement: "Lord...if you had been here, my brother would not have died." Four things can be said about this comment made by Martha and Mary. First, it was a statement of faith. By speaking in this manner to Jesus, they were affirming His power. Not only that, but also they called Him "Lord." Paul said, "No one can say, 'Jesus is Lord,' except by the Holy Spirit" (1 Cor. 12:3). Martha and Mary therefore uttered a statement of faith.

It was also a statement of fact. You can mark it; had Jesus

been there personally and observed Lazarus's illness, He would have healed Lazarus. Lazarus would certainly not have died.

It was also a statement of feeling. It came from the heart of hearts. All they were doing was expressing deep feeling. And believers are always entitled to express their hearts to God. After all, the Lord knows everything in our hearts (Heb. 4:13). Moreover, our Lord is touched with the feeling of our weaknesses (Heb. 4:15).

I know this about my Lord Jesus Christ: I can say anything to Him. I can talk to Him about anything and express any feeling that I have. If I were to say what I feel to you, it might hurt you. It may not be good for you to know I had a particular feeling. But Jesus allows me to express my feelings to Him.

There are times when we need to express what we feel— to someone. Earlier I talked about repression, denying what we truly feel. This is almost always a bad thing to do. The worst thing in the world is to not be able to express a feeling. It may be a bizarre feeling, yes. It may be misguided. It may be ill conceived. It may be quite unjustified. But if you feel it, it does you no good to repress it—to push it down into the cellar of unconsciousness. It is not healthy, neither physically nor emotionally. Repression can be the cause of any number of physical or psychological illnesses. Many times people have illnesses that are traceable to repressed feelings.

A Statement of Familiarity

If there is no one on this earth we can turn to (lest they make us feel even worse), we can always turn to Jesus. We can say *anything* to Him. Martha did just that: "Lord...if you had been here, my brother would not have died." A few moments later, Mary came with the same comment. It was as though they rehearsed it together. You can be sure they discussed it and agreed on it. If anything in the world was obvious to them, it was this. It was a statement of fact but also of feeling.

And yet it was also a statement of familiarity. It shows that they already had a relationship with Jesus. We might think that this was impertinent language. But they were not being impertinent because they knew Him very well. They knew they could talk like this to Him.

Martha felt so free in uttering these words to Jesus that she did not bother to wait for His response. She just kept talking. "Lord...if you had been here, my brother would not have died. But I know that even now God will give you whatever you ask" (John 11:21–22). It was a familial relationship that she had with our Lord.

In Mary's case, the same thing is quickly seen. When Mary saw Jesus, she fell down at His feet and sobbed her heart out. "Lord, if you had been here, my brother would not have died" (v. 32). When would anyone do a thing like that? Only when a previous relationship of considerable consequence existed. Mary had a lot to express. She did it nonverbally and verbally. However bitter she felt, she knew that somehow it was safe to be herself with Jesus.

This then is how a believer can talk to the Lord. We may be wrong in our attitude, but we know, nonetheless, that we can express our feelings. When we are not in the best frame of mind, we can turn to Jesus. He never scolds or moralizes.

Do you know this Jesus? Do you have a friend like Him? Do you know one who will accept you as you are?

COULD NOT *THIS MAN*...?

We turn to the second statement: "Could not he who opened the eyes of the blind man have kept this man from dying?" (John 11:37). This clearly is an utterance of some people who do not know or care about Jesus. Certain things can be said about this statement. It was a statement of detachment. With Martha and Mary, it was calling Him "Lord." But verse 37 says, "But some of them said, 'Could not he who opened the eyes...'" As the King James Version puts it, "Could not *this man*...?" (emphasis added).

They were detached from Jesus. It was as though they were talking to each other and nodding their heads toward where Jesus was standing, saying, "Could not this man have caused that Lazarus had not died?" In other words, there was an utter lack of personal concern and involvement. Martha and Mary called Him "Lord." Those wishing to criticize called Him "this man." People who speak in the latter manner speak this way about God when they really have no vital interest in wanting to know Him or understand Him.

Which attitude is yours? Will you acknowledge Jesus as *Lord*, or do you just glance over your shoulder and refer to Him as *that man*? Are you so detached that you are in fact looking for an excuse not to believe? That is why some of them reacted to Lazarus's death and Jesus as they did. They wanted to be confirmed in their preconceptions about Jesus.

They did not want to believe Him in the first place. The easy way out was to stay detached and refer glibly to "this man."

It was equally a statement of derogation. What some of those present wanted to do was to detract from the power and integrity of Jesus. "Could not he who opened the eyes of the blind man have kept this man from dying?" Rather than affirm His power for what He was able to do, they wanted to cast doubt on His integrity for what He didn't do.

But in speaking like this, they actually condemned themselves. For they acknowledged what Jesus had done elsewhere. "Could not he who opened the eyes of the blind...?" How did they know that Jesus opened the eyes of blind people? If they knew that Jesus did that sort of thing, then they were without excuse for speaking about Him like that. They clearly acknowledged what He had done. Why would anyone speak in a derogatory manner about someone who healed blind people?

I suspect there are a lot of church members who have spoken this way about God. They are in the church, have been baptized, and have a good reputation in the community, but they are detached from the Lord in their hearts and have actually spoken about God in a derogatory manner.

Unsaved Church Members

When I was witnessing as a Pilot Light on the streets of England, I talked with hundreds of people on the steps of Westminster Chapel who admitted to being church members. But when I spoke to them about their relationship with Jesus

Christ, they often spewed out the most unkind hostilities toward God. They spoke exactly like some of those who saw Jesus at the tomb of Lazarus. Even though they were church members, they began to complain about what God didn't do here or there in the world. They showed nothing but hate for God when they spoke in this manner. Some of them gave mental assent to Jesus's death and resurrection—but would not confess Him as their Lord.

Are you a church member who is not saved? "Surely this is not possible," you will say. But it is. It is very possible. It is also very common. What a pity, what a tragedy, if you trust your church membership and vague knowledge about God and the Bible and end up in a Godless eternity. It doesn't need to happen to you. You may be a very "good" person, that is, a very moral person. But morality does not save. There are Hindus and Muslims who are just as moral as you. Do you really believe that good works earn you a place in heaven?

Which would you rather do: derogate the Son of God or dignify Him? When something happens that you don't understand, would you detract from the integrity of Christ or dignify Him?

The statement of some of those near the tomb of Lazarus was a statement of defiance. All they wanted to do was to voice their contempt for Jesus. This is what rolled out of their hearts. Jesus said, "For out of the overflow of the heart the mouth speaks.... I tell you that men will have to give account on the day of judgment for every careless word they have spoken" (Matt. 12:34, 36).

HE WHO IS UNJUST IN THE LEAST

It is possible to be moral outwardly but inwardly feel defiant about Jesus Christ. You may not be engaged in immorality—adultery, homosexuality, pornography, lying, killing. You may be an honest person but inwardly feel nothing but contempt for Jesus Christ.

Those who uttered this statement about Jesus were in all probability very moral men. They were in good standing with the "authorities" in Israel who were waiting and watching to get something to accuse Jesus. As they were building their case against Jesus, rather than bow at His feet, they confirmed themselves in their unbelief.

This is why people would rather hear some scientific word that supports evolution rather than a biblical sermon on the Creation story in Genesis. People want to be able to laugh about the Genesis account of Creation. When a scientist begins to question the theory of evolution (and it is happening all the time in ever-increasing numbers), it gives people a very restless, uneasy feeling. They much prefer to gather evidence that justifies their hostility against God.

Here were men who, by their own statement, acknowledged the good that Jesus had done: "He healed the blind." Surely the most rational and sensible thing they could have done—minimally—was to wait and see what Jesus might do next. They might have lowered their voices. They might have approached Him with nothing but deepest respect. A man with such authority over nature and demons surely deserves anyone's respect.

But sin in us transcends common sense. Sin in us justifies our feelings against God. Rather than wait, ponder, consider, investigate, and contemplate the claims of Jesus Christ, we hastily confirm ourselves in what it is we hope to be true.

It is really a very dangerous thing to speak defiantly about Jesus, who Himself said, "He that is faithful in that which is least is faithful also in much: and he that is unjust in the least is unjust also in much" (Luke 16:10, KJV). Later we will examine the reaction of these men after Jesus's motives became apparent. In other words, we will see whether the unveiling of Christ's ultimate purpose and power made any difference in their attitude toward Him. "He that is unjust in the least is unjust also in much." The Bible says, "Kiss the Son, lest he be angry and you be destroyed in your way, for his wrath can flare up in a moment" (Ps. 2:12).

JESUS LISTENS

The final thing that must be said about the statement of those men is this: it was a statement of declaration. They wanted to voice publicly where they stood with regard to Jesus of Nazareth. They chose to declare themselves.

It is amazing—is it not?—how the world is unashamed to voice its contempt for Jesus Christ! Look at the articles that manage to find their way into secular magazines and newspapers. I receive a famous newspaper every day through the mail. There is often a religious article in it. It is an exceedingly rare day when there is an article that reflects either a true biblical position or one reflecting the gospel. It is often an article that borders on contempt for the God of the Bible and the historic Christian faith.

Despite my academic credentials and my history of being a pastor, such newspapers and magazines would not be very interested in the contribution I might make. But if I were to present an article in which I confessed that I no longer believed in the Virgin Birth of Christ, atonement by Christ's blood, conversion by faith alone, and eternal hell, I have a feeling this would be acceptable. This media seem totally open to what is agnostic or contemptuous of simple faith in this Bible.

Those near the tomb of Lazarus wanted to declare themselves. They were happy to be overheard. They were not ashamed to criticize Jesus, even though He had healed the blind in previous days.

Does Jesus care? How does He feel when people speak to Him as Martha and Mary did or as the unbelievers did? How does He react?

Jesus listens. Can there be a more wonderful experience in the world than to have the attention of Jesus? There are prominent people who exercise considerable influence in the world and who are sought after by many people; one hopes for a precious five minutes with such personalities. What it would mean to someone to have the president stop and chat with them on one of his outings; the same as someone in England might feel to have an audience with Her Majesty the Queen! Often two minutes would do. They just want to be heard.

Jesus listens. I would love to interview people who have talked with Jesus. I would want to ask, "What was He really like? Did He look you right in the eyes? Did His mind seem to be preoccupied? Did He breathe a sigh because you stopped and asked Him a question? Did He seem in a hurry? Did He really listen? Did He take in what you said? What was His reaction?" After all, you can tell whether a person cares by the look in his eyes. "What was the look in Jesus's eyes? Tell me, did you get the impression in your heart of hearts whether He actually cared?"

Martha was not content merely to say, "If You had been here, my brother would not have died." She kept on talking. But Jesus kept on listening. He had all day for Martha—and Mary. And for whoever wanted Him.

I heard Arthur Blessitt preach a sermon once in England's Westminster Chapel on the subject, "Getting Through to Jesus." He made the point that those who *want* to get through to Jesus *do* get to Him.

Those who really wanted to get to Jesus succeeded. Once, they had to dig a hole in the roof of a house where Jesus happened to be, then dropped a lame man practically in Jesus's lap! But they were intent on getting through to Jesus.

Find Jesus. For when you find Him, He listens—carefully, earnestly, compassionately.

Why do you suppose the poor loved Him so much? Why did the common people hear Him gladly? What was it about Jesus that convinced the leper (rejected by all society) he could get away with rushing up to Jesus, falling before Him, and pleading, "Lord, if you are willing, you can make me clean" (Matt. 8:2)? Those who saw Jesus recognized Him as one who cared. How did He show it? By listening.

A little girl once said to me, "My daddy loves me."

I said, "Really? How do you know he loves you?"

She replied, "Because he spends time with me." Nothing haunts me more than the painful memories of my being preoccupied with what I felt I had to do while my two children grew up right under my nose. If I could relive those years, I would take more time with my children and be careful to listen to them.

Jesus listens. He does not make us feel unimportant. He does not treat our feelings with insensitivity. He does not make us feel stupid for what we think, feel, or ask. What an honor it would have been to have a personal conversation with Jesus of Nazareth.

And yet, we can. Absolutely. I don't understand it, but even though millions may be talking to Him at once—through the miracle of the Holy Spirit who came to take His place (John 14:16)—we can talk to Jesus as though He were in the room with us. Sometimes He makes His presence known by the power of the Holy Spirit so that you want to reach out and touch Him. I'm serious. I am not exaggerating one bit. There have been times when Jesus was more real to me than any person around me.

What a great listener Jesus is. He gives you His undivided attention. His mind will never wander as you talk to Him. He will never be bored with your conversation. St. Augustine said that God loves every man as though there were no one else to love. Jesus listens to every man or woman as though there were no one else to listen to. He will never rap on the table and say, "Get on with it. I don't have much time," as I fear I have done at times when people wanted to see me.

JESUS SEES YOU

Jesus looks. After Mary said to Jesus, "Lord, if you had been here, my brother would not have died," the next verse shows that "Jesus *saw* her weeping..." (John 11:33, emphasis added).

It would have been a marvel just to see Jesus in the flesh. I have seen a few famous people in the world. I remember the first president I saw. It was Harry S. Truman when he was running for the presidency in 1948. His train came through Ashland, Kentucky. He appeared at the rear. I was with thousands of other people. When he walked out from behind the velvet curtain, all of us began to wave at him, hoping he would look directly at us. I kept hoping that he would see me.

A friend of mine was in a crowd that saw Senator John F. Kennedy when he first ran for presidency. She claims that when the senator's car came along, he looked straight at her. She was dazzled for days. It was one thing to have seen John F. Kennedy, but another that he saw her!

Greater than seeing Jesus is knowing that He sees us. "Jesus saw her weeping." It was more important to Mary that He noticed her than it was for her to see Him. But He did see her. He saw her weeping. That was all she really wanted at that moment anyway, just to be seen as she was. She was distraught that Jesus should have stayed away. She was deeply hurt that He showed up four days after the funeral.

She wanted Him to know how she felt. She fell at His feet and sobbed. Jesus saw her weeping.

Simon Peter denied knowing Jesus to a little servant girl and then denied Him twice more. Immediately the rooster crowed. "The Lord turned and looked straight at Peter" (Luke 22:61). That was one time that being seen by Jesus was a painful experience. Peter "went outside and wept bitterly" (v. 62).

One of John Newton's greatest hymns begins with the words, "In evil long I took delight." These lines follow:

> Unawed by shame or fear,
> Till a new object struck my sight,
> And stopped my wild career.
>
> I saw One hanging on a tree,
> In agony and blood;
> He fixed His languid eyes on me,
> As near His cross I stood.
>
> Sure, never, till my latest breath,
> Can I forget that look:
> It seemed to charge me with His death,
> Tho' not a word He spoke.
>
> A second look He gave, which said,
> "I freely all forgive:
> This blood is for thy ransom paid,
> I die that thou may'st live."[1]
>
> —JOHN NEWTON

Jesus looks. We want to know that He is aware of what we are feeling. Does He know what I am feeling? Does He know when I'm sad? Does He know when I'm lonely? And does He care? Yes. He looks. He sees. He doesn't turn His head from our plight. He does not look the other way. "Jesus saw her weeping." He looks.

I CALL THAT LOVE

That is not all. Jesus loves. "When Jesus saw her weeping, and the Jews who had come along with her also weeping, he was deeply moved in spirit and troubled" (John 11:33). He was affected by their hurt. He let Himself get involved. Why? He loved Mary and Martha.

> But what to those who find? Ah, this
> Nor tongue nor pen can show;
> The love of Jesus, what it is,
> None but His loved ones know.[2]
> —BERNARD OF CLAIRVAUX AND EDWARD CASWALL

Jesus felt what they were feeling and entered into their sorrow, even though He knew that in moments the whole situation would be changed. But He knew that *they* did not know that. He lived with them fully in the present.

That is the way Jesus loves. He is not like an annoyed parent who will say, "Stop crying. You'll feel better tomorrow." Rather, our Lord lives in the exact present as though there were no tomorrow.

This, to me, is one of the most astonishing things about God. Why would He waste time comforting me with His presence and any number of verses from His Word when He already knows that I may soon feel better anyway? I saw this as most extraordinary. The God who knows the happy outcome lives with me in the very present moment to comfort me as though He had nothing on His mind but my feelings at the time. I call that love.

When we are feeling hurt and bewildered over our Lord's delay in answering our prayers, He has a way of coming alongside and putting His loving arms around us—and weeps with us. "Jesus wept" (John 11:35). "A bruised reed he will not break" (Matt. 12:20). When He sees us weeping, He weeps too. If you want to make a friend for life, let another who is crying see *your* tears. Whatever bitterness Mary felt for the previous four days was now dissolved into sheer gratitude. Once she saw how Jesus really felt, I promise you, she did not care what His reasons were for tarrying. His caring presence sent a signal to her that whatever He was up to was right and whatever reason for His delay did not matter. Seeing how much He cared now solved her whole problem.

EVERYTHING AFFECTS GOD

I now turn to the other comment, "Could not he who opened the eyes of the blind man have kept this man from dying?" (John 11:37). Did Jesus care when this utterance was made?

Jesus refused to respond to their question. He mirrored God's silence when it comes to answering this kind of question. But it does not mean He does not care.

The next sentence says, "Jesus, once more deeply moved, came to the tomb" (John 11:38). The King James Version says, "groaning in himself"! This tells me that Jesus *felt* what they said but ignored it. He heard it. He knew what they meant by it. He was not unaffected by it. But He ignored it.

When God hears people utter contemptible things about Himself, what does He do about it? He hears His name taken in vain. He hears disgraceful things said about His beloved Son. He hears awful things said about His beloved church—the apple of His eye. Why doesn't He step down from heaven and strike people dead who speak about Him like this? Doesn't He care? If God cared about this, surely He would show it (we may think).

He ignores it, but He cares. He groans within Himself. He hears and feels it. But He goes on with His purpose in the world. He has a plan. In a little while, all will see what He was up to. The same God who weeps when we weep equally groans when scoffers utter ridicule toward His Son, but He ignores it and gets on with His perfect plan.

As I mentioned before, I recall hearing a minister say things over the radio that to me were virtually blasphemous. How disgraceful it was for a minister to speak as this one did! I thought, "God, why do You let this go on? Don't You care?"

We should never take God's silence as a signal from heaven that He does not care. We should let Jesus's groaning be a loud signal as to how deeply our Lord feels when He is charged with the troubles of the world.

In any case, time is on God's side. He is in no hurry to expose the hearts of men. This will come in due course. Incidentally, the radio minister referred to above was found dead a few years later in a San Francisco hotel and was seen by many to have been the fraud he was.

God's silence does not mean He does not care. *Everything*

affects God. Let no one think that people dying in their sins and being sent to eternal doom are carried out impassively by God. "Have I any pleasure at all that the wicked should die?...I have no pleasure in the death of him that dieth, saith the Lord GOD" (Ezek. 18:23, 32, KJV).

Because He does care.

6

DOES JESUS CARE WHEN WE ACKNOWLEDGE HIS POWER?

While Alexi Bischkov was the General Secretary of Baptists of the Soviet Union, he made a very interesting observation about Christianity in Russia vis-à-vis his observations in Britain and America. He stated that he thought Christianity in the West is largely patterned after Martha, whereas in Russia, Christianity is more like Mary.

On one occasion, Jesus went to the home of Mary and Martha to be given hospitality by them. As soon as Jesus arrived, Mary was at His feet, "listening to what he said. But Martha was distracted by all the preparations that had to be made" (Luke 10:39–40). She no doubt was annoyed with Mary for spending her time with Jesus rather than getting things ready, but it was Jesus to whom she made her feelings known. "Lord, don't you care that my sister has left me to do the work by myself? Tell her to help me!" (v. 40). But Jesus refused to rebuke Mary for her desire to spend all her time sitting at His feet. He said instead, "Martha, Martha...you are worried and upset about many things, but only one thing is needed. Mary has chosen what is better, and it will not be taken away from her" (v. 41–42).

Mr. Bischkov's observation of Christians in the West is that they are "careful and troubled about many things," as the King James Version translates the passage above. He thinks that we in the West are bogged down by organization and preparation for spiritual things while Christians in Russia merely want to spend time in the presence of the Lord. Having spent two weeks in what was the Soviet Union in 1985, visiting a number of their churches and getting to know many Christians, I would concur with his statement. I detected a level of genuine piety and devotion to the person of Jesus there that I have seldom found anywhere else. Christians in the former Soviet Union had a simple dependence on the Lord Jesus and an experiential knowledge of Him that moved my wife and me very deeply indeed.

Luke's account of Martha and Mary provides us with a further insight into their personalities. It will be recalled that it was Mary who fell at Jesus's feet and cried when He turned up four days after Lazarus's funeral. It was Martha who first met Jesus when He approached their home, "...but Mary stayed at home" (John 11:20). Mary may have been sulking. Perhaps she felt that her devotion to Christ gave her a certain claim on Him. It is also possible that she had been more devoted to Him. But perhaps it was also that she was more intense than Martha and her feelings went deeper.

If Mary was the more intense, Martha was probably the more intellectual. Martha apparently was more theologically minded, which suggests she did not spend all her time in the kitchen. The conversation between Jesus and Martha shows that she had absorbed some of Jesus's teachings in considerable depth. It is not unusual that two sisters are opposites. The younger sister is frequently quite different from the older one, and the difference is often seen in terms of who is the more cerebral and who is the more emotional.

BUT I KNOW...

When Martha heard that Jesus was coming, she went out to meet Him. She said, "Lord...if you had been here, my brother would not have died. But I know that even now God will give you whatever you ask" (John 11:21–22). Martha shows that in her sorrow, she still has assurance. "But I know..."

It is a wonderful thing to be able to say, "But I know..." in a time of distress. Martha had an abiding faith that kept her in touch with the living God in her time of sorrow. This is because she knew something *before* sorrow came. This comes by hearing the words of Jesus and putting them into practice. Whoever does this, Jesus said, "...is like a wise man who built his house on the rock. The rain came down, the streams rose, and the winds blew and beat against that house; yet it did not fall, because it had its foundation on the rock" (Matt. 7:24–25).

We never know when trouble will come. When it does come, it tests us by causing what we are to come to light. If we hear the teachings of Jesus but do not put them into practice in our experiences, we shall be like what our Lord called "a foolish man who built his house on sand. The rain came down, the streams rose, and the winds blew and beat against that house, and it fell with a great crash" (vv. 26–27).

Can you say, "But I know..." when trouble comes to you? I should like to think this would be the greatest benefit to be derived from reading this book. The Bible says we can *know* certain things. For example, do you *know* that you are saved? Do you *know* that, were you to die today, you would go to heaven? One of the reasons for the Bible being written was that you might know this. "I write these things to you who believe in the name of the Son of God so that you may *know* that you have eternal life" (1 John 5:13, emphasis added).

I have talked to dozens of people from England to the United States who look at me and say, with total honesty, "No one can know for sure that they will go to heaven when they die." But he can! She can! This is why Jesus died on the cross, rose from the dead, ascended to God's right hand, and sent the Holy Spirit! It is the Holy Spirit who convinces you that the Bible is the Word of God. Once you believe the Bible, you can know that you are saved. For this is what the Bible teaches: "I know whom I have believed, and am convinced that he is able to guard what I have entrusted to him for that day" (2 Tim. 1:12). Jesus said, "I tell you the truth, whoever hears my word and believes him who sent me has eternal life and will not be condemned; he has crossed over from death to life" (John 5:24).

How could Martha say, "But I know..."? Because of what she believed to be true about Jesus. "But I know that even now God will give you whatever you ask" (John 11:22). Her trust was not in herself; it was utterly in Jesus. The ability to say, "I know," is not given to a person because of any strength or power within. It is based on a strength and power outside ourselves. Most people think that assurance of salvation is presumptuous. It is quite the opposite. If my assurance of salvation was based on myself and my good works, then, yes, such assurance would be in vain presumption. But my assurance is not in me. It is in Christ—Christ alone.

> My hope is built on nothing less
> Than Jesus' blood and righteousness;
> I dare not trust the sweetest frame,
> But wholly lean on Jesus' name.[1]
>
> —EDWARD MOTE

The ability to say, "I know," derives from the fact of seeing Jesus as all sufficient. It is not a strong faith that saves, but faith in a strong God! When Martha said to Jesus, "Even now God will give you whatever you ask," she was affirming what *Jesus* could do, not what she could do. That is the faith by which a person is justified—regarded as righteous before God. Faith counts for righteousness (Rom. 4:5). Faith perceives its object—Jesus Christ. That was the faith Martha had and the reason she could say "I know..."

HONORING JESUS

What Martha was doing, then, was acknowledging Jesus's power. She was honoring Jesus. "Those who honor me I will honor," God says (1 Sam. 2:30). Jesus said, "Moreover, the Father judges no one, but has entrusted all judgment to the Son, that all may honor the Son just as they honor the Father" (John 5:22–23). If God could say, "Those who honor me, I will honor," and if Jesus could say, "All may honor the Son just as they honor the Father," then it shows that if we will honor Jesus, He will honor us!

There is no higher thing to do than to honor Jesus Christ. Even Jesus's inner circle—Peter, James, and John—had to be taught this. One day Jesus took them up to a high mountain. While there, Jesus "...was transfigured before them. His face shone like the sun, and his clothes became as white as the light" (Matt. 17:2). At that point Moses and Elijah appeared and talked with Jesus. Peter, partly from fear and excitement, and most certainly without the leadership of the Holy Spirit, said, "Lord, it is good for us to be here. If you wish, I will put up three shelters—one for you, one for Moses and one for Elijah" (v. 4). At this stage Peter naïvely thought that Jesus was equal to, but no greater than, Moses and Elijah. But while Peter "was still speaking, a bright cloud enveloped them, and a voice from the cloud said, 'This is my Son, whom I love; with him I am well pleased. Listen to him!' When the disciples heard this, they fell facedown to the ground, terrified" (vv. 5–6). Jesus touched them and said, "Get up...Don't be afraid" (v. 7). And "When they looked up, they saw no one except Jesus" (v. 8).

When Martha said to Jesus, "I know that even now God will give you whatever you ask" (John 11:22), she acknowledged His authority. Jesus had once said, "For as the Father has life in himself, so he has granted the Son to have life in himself. And he has given him authority to judge because he is the Son of Man" (John 5:26–27). He said that He had authority to lay down His life "and authority to take it up again" (John 10:18). The Father granted Jesus "authority over all people that he might give eternal life to all those" the Father gave Him (John 17:2).

THE FAITH OF JESUS

What Martha perceived, moreover, was Jesus's authority with the Father because of His knowledge of the Father. Here is a simple but very important truth: Jesus knew God. J. I. Packer has written a classic titled *Knowing God*.[2] Jesus prayed that His own "may know you, the only true God, and Jesus Christ, whom you have sent" (John 17:3). It is a marvelous thing to know God, and yet Jesus said, "No one knows the Son except the Father, and no one knows the Father except the Son and those to whom the Son chooses to reveal him" (Matt. 11:27). The only way we can know God, then, is by Jesus's own prerogative, by His initiative and power.

Martha, therefore, knew that Jesus knew the Father. And yet, what Jesus said in the above verses shows us that Martha's very faith was but the consequence of Jesus's power. All this is very humbling. It shows us that we are what we are by the grace of God, including the ability to believe and perceive

Jesus's power. John the Baptist testified, "A man can receive only what is given him from heaven" (John 3:27). To put it another way, Martha's acknowledgment of Jesus's power shows the work of the Holy Spirit in her.

Jesus said, "The Spirit gives life; the flesh counts for nothing" (John 6:63). This means that in ourselves—what Jesus called "flesh"—is no inherent ability to believe or perceive spiritual things. Jesus went on to say, "No one can come to me unless the Father has enabled him" (v. 65). Therefore Martha's very coming to Jesus was nothing more than the prompting of the Spirit, not to mention the things she perceived about Jesus.

Martha acknowledged Jesus's power in prayer. "I know that even now God will give you whatever you ask" (John 11:22). This tells us something more about Jesus—that He was a man of prayer. When He prayed, it was with a perfect faith. John the Baptist also said that God gave His Holy Spirit to Jesus "without limit" (John 3:34). To each of us is given a certain "measure of faith" (Rom. 12:3). So there are limits to our faith; we are given faith in measure. There were no limits to Jesus's faith. He was given faith without measure. Martha perceived this about Jesus. She knew that Jesus could ask for anything—and get it.

Do you perceive this about Jesus? When you do, your spiritual life will "take off." It is an emancipating experience for the one who comes to see, understand, and trust the *faith of Jesus*. I suspect this is one of the greater truths of the New Testament: the faith of Jesus. People either underestimate or forget entirely that Jesus had faith. When the ancient prophet said, "I will put my trust in him" (Isa. 8:17), he was speaking of Jesus's own faith, according to the writer of the epistle to the Hebrews (Heb. 2:13).

The implications of this truth are profound. Two things need to be stressed in any case. First, the faith of Jesus was the very foundation of Paul's doctrine of justification by faith. It is here that we must appeal to the King James Version, which simply translates rather than interprets the Greek (as opposed to some modern translations). Paul said the righteousness of God is by the "faith of Jesus Christ unto all and upon all them that believe" (Rom. 3:22, KJV). As our substitute, Jesus believed for us—perfectly. He also obeyed for us—perfectly (Rom. 5:19). But all that Jesus did and suffered for us is of no value unless we ourselves believe. This is why Paul said that the righteousness (or justice) of God is by Jesus Christ's own faith to all, and upon all, them that believe. It is for *all*, yes, but all who *believe*. The faith of Jesus alone is not enough. Jesus too had to believe.

Paul states this precise truth in Galatians, "We have believed in Jesus Christ, that we might be justified by the faith of Christ" (Gal. 2:16, KJV). The foundation, then, is Christ's faith. What guarantees salvation is that the faith of Christ is an accomplished fact. We who believe do so in order that we might be justified by Christ's own faith. Otherwise Paul is speaking redundantly. I fear that the translators of these verses (and others) have not had sufficient understanding of this blessed truth by which they might have seen the utter simplicity of the Greek phrase *pistis christou* (literally, "faith of Christ"). It is the only way to make complete sense of Paul's doctrine of justification generally and the humanity of Christ particularly. This is repeated in Galatians 3:22 (KJV).

THROUGH HIS FAITH

The second important reason for stressing this has to do with our own prayer lives. When we perceive our Lord Jesus Christ at God's right hand, we need to understand He is interceding for us with a perfect faith. Yes, He prays for us, but with a measure of doubt? Absolutely not! His intercessory work is absolute. How do I know that I should be kept until the last day? Because Jesus has promised to pray for me until the end! Am I depending on *my* faith—or His? Let Paul's answer be yours: "The life which I now live in the flesh I live by the faith of the Son of God" (Gal. 2:20, KJV). The Greek literally translated is, "I live in faith [namely] that of the Son of God." Great though Paul's own faith was (I suspect), he did not live by his own faith. His faith, or trust, was in Jesus's faith. That is precisely where Martha stood in her relationship to Jesus. She just put the focus on Him. It is this understanding of our relationship to Christ that will actually enable us to cast all our care on Him who cares for us (1 Pet. 5:7).

In 1977, our family lived in England but moved to Ealing, a borough in Greater London, when I accepted the call to pastor at Westminster Chapel. This meant moving our children into another school. It was a very stressful time for all of us, not the least of which concerned my son TR. (We call him TR although he is named after me. Two RTs in the family brought endless confusion, so we took a friend's suggestion and began calling him TR.) As I drove him to his new school on the morning of the first day, he was very nervous and afraid. He simply could not bear the thought of another new teacher, another new playground, or another new bunch of students. He refused to get out of the car. I said, "TR, you'll have to go." He wouldn't move. I said, "Son, look at me. I promise you, I will be praying for you *all day long*. At any moment when you get scared, just remember in that precise moment, Daddy will be praying for you. All day long." He opened the door, got out, and started walking toward the new playground. He never looked back. He wasn't trusting his own faith; he was trusting my faith. He reckoned that somehow his dad's prayers got through to heaven.

Paul made this precise point when he said, "In whom we have boldness and access with confidence by the faith of him" (Eph. 3:12, KJV), (Gr. *dia tes pisteos autou*, "through the faith of him," or "his faith"). It is a clear reference to our Lord's faith. It is what is at work when we pray, whether or not we acknowledge this fact. How much more blessed to know what lies at the foundation of effectual praying!

It is not great faith that saves, only faith in a great Savior. This is true at the point of conversion and also in the living of the Christian life. It is why, then, we are given leave to cast our burden on the Lord and find that He sustains us (Ps. 55:22).

LORD, IF YOU ARE WILLING

Martha also acknowledged Jesus's sovereignty. Now the word *sovereignty* obviously has more than one meaning. But in this case it refers to one's sovereign prerogative to give or withhold a favor. That belongs to royalty, does it not? A sovereign has the right to determine who comes into his or her presence. Jesus had this kind of power—to exercise it or not to do so. He could command if He chose to do so. Martha knew the kind of influence Jesus had with the Father. But it was up to Jesus whether He would turn to the Father or not.

To put it another way, Martha was letting Jesus be Himself. "Whatever You ask, God will give it"—if. It was a big *if*. If You choose to ask, Lord, You will get it. But Martha was allowing our Lord to make the final decision as to whether or not He put a request through to God the Father. She acknowledged Jesus's own right to the Father but equally His right not to turn to the Father.

The leper who came to Jesus had the same faith: "Lord, if you are willing, you can make me clean" (Matt. 8:2). The faith that the leper had was in Jesus's power but equally in His sovereign prerogative to give or withhold mercy. "Jesus reached out his hand and touched the man. 'I am willing,' he said. 'Be clean!' Immediately he was cured" (v. 3).

May I suggest this way of approaching the Lord to you? Are you like so many of us—at least when we first seek God— who fancy that we are doing God some kind of a favor by even coming to Him? I must say that when we approach Him in a rather patronizing manner, it betrays that we have *not* seen His power and authority. For when we see Jesus as He really is, we will realize what an infinite favor He has bestowed on us when we turn to Him at all.

All that Martha saw and acknowledged in Jesus may be

summed up in one word: *power*. She acknowledged His power. She knew that Jesus could do anything. She knew that if Jesus decided to do it, He could raise Lazarus from the dead at that very moment. Raising Lazarus from the dead was what Martha in fact hoped for. She all but said this. She veiled her explicit request by merely saying, "God will give you whatever *you* ask" (John 11:22, emphasis added). He knew what she hoped for. She knew that He knew what she hoped for. At this stage, Jesus decided to test her faith. He said, "'Your brother will rise again.' Martha answered, 'I know he will rise again in the resurrection at the last day'" (vv. 23–24). It is difficult to know why Martha answered like that. Perhaps it was because she feared that Jesus *wouldn't* raise Lazarus then, and she wanted to acknowledge that it may well have been the Lord's will not to do it. I doubt that her reason for saying that was merely to affirm her orthodoxy. With some people, I fear that their entire outlook is but eschatological— that is, they don't expect God to do anything now but only in the last day. Martha was saying, "Yes, Lord, I know that my brother will be raised at the last day—of course I believe that. But isn't there something You might be willing to do *now*?" This to me is what lay behind her comment.

Martha may therefore have thought that Jesus's statement, "Your brother will rise again," was His way of saying, "I'm sorry, Martha. You will have to wait until the last day before you see your brother again." If that is what Jesus meant, then Martha was prepared to go along with that as well.

But here was a robust faith at work. She believed all the necessary things one should believe about "last things." But her faith was not merely in what God will do by-and-by; she believed God was able to do something *now*.

Does Jesus care when we acknowledge His power? Does He care when we have a faith like that of Martha?

Most of us protect ourselves by affirming our orthodoxy rather than our simple faith that God will act in the here and now. I sometimes wonder if our orthodoxy is but a camouflage for our unbelief. Because we don't really believe that God will work today, we take refuge in what He will do tomorrow.

There are those who believe that God *once* worked powerfully in men's lives. When? In the days of the early church. They therefore believe in the Book of Acts with all their hearts. They believe in the miracles of Jesus. They believe in His resurrection. They believe in His ascension. They believe in His intercessory work at God's right hand. They are orthodox, yes. But that is about all. Their faith in God's power is either limited to the distant past or the last day. In between, it is mostly soundness of doctrine that counts.

Most of us are afraid to put ourselves on the line as Martha did. We don't want to look like fools. We content ourselves with the orthodox statement, "I know He will rise again in the Resurrection at the last day." It is like those who state the Apostles' Creed. That seems to be the extent of their faith. What God *did* and *will do*.

What zeal Martha had! Many of us would stand on the sidelines and say, "I'm not going to be found talking to the Lord like that. After all, if God wants to do something, fine. No need to be so unsubtle about what we hope God will do. Let God do it if that is what He wants to do."

Not Martha. This dear child of God saw in Jesus the power to do something *on the spot*.

DO YOU BELIEVE THIS?

Does Jesus care when we acknowledge His power like that?

He does. How does He show it? *He affirms such faith when He sees it in us.* Jesus said to Martha, "I am the resurrection and the life. He who believes in me will live, even though he dies; and whoever lives and believes in me will never die. *Do you believe this?*" (John 11:25–26, emphasis added). Jesus revealed verbally to Martha what she already knew in her heart to be true. She had not articulated it in those precise words, but it described her faith exactly. By stating it as He did, Jesus gave her yet another opportunity to confess Him. What He said He had not said before, and yet what He said fills out what had to be true about Him. Jesus let Martha know exactly what was true about Himself and gave her the privilege of affirming this fuller revelation.

Jesus said if we are faithful in that which is least, we will be faithful in that which is much (Luke 16:10, KJV). The "much" in this case was the fuller revelation of Jesus to Martha. She could accept it because she had been faithful in the "least" all along. She was "troubled about many things," but she did not lag behind in her trust in Jesus's power. When she heard a fuller revelation of Jesus's power, it added up to what she knew must be true.

When we are walking in the light we already have, God's guidance into greater truth and understanding will come readily. We shall be fully ready for the next layer of truth.

The proof that we have the "real thing" is that we shall affirm everything the Bible continues to say about Jesus. Perhaps it was not explicit in our minds at first. But it will eventually be. Those who have a true faith in Jesus will not draw back from all else that can be revealed about Him.

Does Jesus care when we acknowledge His power? Yes. He affirms such faith. He does not leave us high and dry. He does not let us be put to shame. Others may not have dreamed of believing God could do something extraordinary immediately, but Martha followed her heart—which was nothing less than the leadership of the Spirit.

Thus Jesus gave her the very words she wanted to hear: "I am the resurrection and the life....*Do you believe this*?" (John 11:25–26, emphasis added). He gave her opportunity to deny this if she could no longer accept it. But there was no problem. None at all. "'Yes, Lord,' she told him. 'I believe that you are the Christ, the Son of God, who was to come into the world'" (v. 27).

What joy Martha must have been experiencing about this time. She was not put to shame for such "impertinence" as fancying that Jesus might raise her brother from the dead. Jesus affirmed such simple, childlike faith. "And without faith it is impossible to please God, because anyone who comes to him must believe that he exists and that he rewards those who earnestly seek him" (Heb. 11:6).

It may mean that we shall have to accept Jesus's rebuke about being "worried and upset about many things." It would seem that Martha accepted that rebuke and that she learned well in the end.

7

DOES JESUS CARE WHEN WE ACKNOWLEDGE HIS DEITY?

T he highest act of worship is to call Jesus "God." But to call Him that would not make Him God. We call Jesus "God" because He is God. If He were not God, calling Jesus "God" would be idolatry.

The most fundamental belief of the Christian faith is the deity of Jesus Christ. *Deity* means God, thus the deity of Christ is a way of saying that Christ, or Jesus, is God.

To acknowledge Jesus as God is not saying that He is "like" God; neither is it saying that Jesus is God's highest creation. We mean that Jesus is very God.

This means that Jesus had no earthly father. The reason that Jesus is called the Son of God is that, though He was man—very man—He had no natural father. He is called the Son of God because the Word, *logos*, became flesh by inhabiting the womb of the Virgin Mary. "In the beginning was the

Word [Greek, *logos*], and the Word was with God, and the Word was God" (John 1:1). The Word that was "with" God, showing a Trinitarian relationship before He entered Mary's womb, was coequal with God and cosubstantial with God from all eternity. The Word impregnated a virgin's womb, namely that of Mary who lived in Nazareth.

When the angel Gabriel came to Mary, he told her that she would become pregnant and give birth to the Son of God. "'How will this be,' Mary asked the angel, 'since I am a virgin?' The angel answered, 'The Holy Spirit will come upon you, and the power of the Most High will overshadow you. So the holy one to be born will be called the Son of God.... For nothing is impossible with God'" (Luke 1:34–35, 37). "The Word became flesh and made his dwelling among us. We have seen his glory, the glory of the One and Only, who came from the Father, full of grace and truth" (John 1:14).

ARE YOU ABLE TO SAY IT?

It is the essential content of a person's profession of faith that he or she testifies that Jesus is God. If someone says, "But I believe everything about Jesus except that," we must politely but candidly say he or she is not a Christian. It is not meant to be unkind when we say this; it is merely stating a fact. The sum of the Christian confession of faith is in Romans 10:9, "If you confess with your mouth, 'Jesus is Lord,' and believe in your heart that God raised him from the dead, you will be saved." If you are unable to say from your heart, "Jesus is Lord," you may be quite honest and straightforward. And I would respect you. But you are also showing that the Holy Spirit has not effectually worked in your heart. This is why Paul said, "No one can say, 'Jesus is Lord,' except by the Holy Spirit" (1 Cor. 12:3). The word *can* comes from a Greek word that means "to be able."

Some people think that it is only the sophisticated intellectual who is unable to say that Jesus is God. Not so. I have watched the simplest people in the world recoil with offense at the thought of admitting that Jesus Christ of Nazareth was God. Whether it be a Muslim or an American living in the Bible Belt of the United States, the *only* thing that will enable a person to grasp and confess from the heart that Jesus is God is the Holy Spirit. If a person reading these lines says, "Oh my, I suppose I'd better start saying it then," I can only point out that perhaps you are not being honest. When Paul talks about believing something in the "heart" (Rom. 10:9), he means that one really *does* believe this: one either does or does not.

As a younger minister, I got the shock of my life one day in 1963. I was pastor of a small church in Carlisle, Ohio. After being there several months, I sensed that there was opposition to my preaching—not because of its style, but because of its content. Various men in the congregation began to object to things that I was saying. But one day the ringleader of the opposition blurted out, "And I don't believe this stuff you've been preaching about Jesus being God, either." Strange as this may seem to the reader, that was one of the happiest things I had heard from that man. For at least I then knew *why* I was being opposed; the man wasn't even a Christian! It is not that

I was glad to find out he was not a Christian (far from it); it was merely that I could at long last understand why he was rejecting all else that I was preaching.

This man had no great intellect. He was a rather simple man, a nice man, and a respectable man in the community. He even believed in the Virgin Birth. But he could not bear my preaching that Jesus was God. To my astonishment, there were ministers in the area who came to that man's aid with the result that I was called before a fraternal order of ministers, the only charge being that I preached "Jesus is God." But those days were good for me. I was driven to the Bible as I had never been before, and I had to come to the point where I was utterly willing to accept exactly what the Bible said on the matter.

The question I raise in this chapter is: Does Jesus care if we acknowledge His deity? Is this something that Jesus Himself wants? Does He *want* us to do it? How important is it that we acknowledge His deity?

So That Others Will Know

The proof that you have been truly converted to Christ by the Holy Spirit is not only that you believe in your heart but that you will confess *with your mouth* that Jesus is God in the flesh. Why with the mouth? So that others will know that you believe it.

Are you ashamed of it? "Whoever acknowledges me before men, I will also acknowledge him before my Father in heaven" (Matt. 10:32). "If anyone is ashamed of me and my words in this adulterous and sinful generation, the Son of Man will be ashamed of him when he comes in his Father's glory with the holy angels" (Mark 8:38).

Perhaps you have wondered whether or not God *has* ever been at work in you. Perhaps you have worried whether or not you are a Christian. Could it be that the devil himself has almost convinced you that you are not the Lord's? Are you wondering if you are one of God's own? I can answer that question for you. It is no guesswork. It is absolutely right. If you are not ashamed to confess that Jesus Christ is God in the flesh, you are a Christian. Worry no more, my dear friend. May God defeat Satan as you read these very lines. May the "accuser of our brethren" be cast down (Rev. 12:10, KJV)!

This is an infallible test. If you, from your heart—without trying to convince yourself by having to look for more evidence or "proofs"—confess that Jesus is God in the flesh, you may know that the blessed Holy Spirit enabled you to do that.

God was at work in Martha. We know that because she acknowledged Jesus's power. Jesus was very pleased with the way she talked to Him.

TO LEAD BY THE HAND

But now Jesus did something that almost moves me to tears. Jesus even wanted Martha to say more. He began to say more about Himself, seeing if she also believed what else was true about Him. "I am the resurrection and the life. He who believes in me will live, even though he dies; and whoever lives and believes in me will never die. Do you believe this?"

(John 11:25–26). Here Martha was led by Jesus's hand, as it were, as He revealed more about Himself.

"Do you believe this?" What Jesus was doing was actually eliciting a confession from her. He knew what was in her heart. He could see that all she affirmed up to then was exactly right. But He wanted her to say *more.* The only way she could say more was to hear more and then respond to what she heard.

What I would like to do in this chapter is to lead you by the hand, as it were, in the hope that I can elicit a confession from you. I only want to bring out what is there, not twist your arm. As we say back in the hills of Kentucky, "A man convinced against his will is of the same opinion still."[1] The proof that a person is really converted is that any further light on essential truth will be met with wholehearted agreement.

When a person is first converted, he may not understand conceptually or verbally all there is to know about Jesus Christ. When one presents the gospel and invites another to receive Christ—no matter how many months one waits before he thinks the time is right—there is still a lot more that he can learn. But if he is truly converted by the Holy Spirit, the same Spirit who enabled him to believe what he *does* understand will open his eyes to all else that is true. He does not reject any further revelation from God's Word when he hears it.

What Martha originally affirmed was good and right. But Jesus wanted to hear more from her. Could that be the case with you?

HIS CLAIM OF DIETY

What else did Jesus say about Himself? He now claimed that *all* resurrection of the dead was His essential work. When Martha stated that Lazarus would be raised on the last day, she was certainly right about that. This in itself is no small bit of truth! Jesus said, "A time is coming when all who are in their graves will hear his voice and come out—those who have done good will rise to live, and those who have done evil will rise to be condemned" (John 5:28–29). Therefore everyone will be raised. Even though our bodies will disintegrate in the process of time after we die, the same God who made our bodies will bring them back, and we will be raised again. But Martha believed that. She believed it already and was not questioning that Lazarus would be raised on the last day.

But Jesus was looking at Martha, possibly with a twinkle in His eye, and saying as it were, "And *who* do you suppose is going to raise Lazarus from the dead in the last day?" This is what Jesus meant by the words, "I am the resurrection and the life." It was His way of saying, "I am the very one who is going to raise Lazarus on the last day. I am behind it all."

This was the first hint that Jesus was prepared to unveil Himself to Martha as being God in the flesh. It was what became orthodoxy after the coming of the Spirit on the Day of Pentecost. Paul wrote, "For by him all things were created: things in heaven and on earth, visible and invisible, whether thrones or powers or rulers or authorities; all things were created by him and for him. He is before all things, and in him all things hold together" (Col. 1:16–17).

It is a hasty assumption by some that Jesus sought to win public approval that He was God. This is simply not true. What is true is that Jesus kept this very truth as best He could from being spread. When an evil spirit cried out, "I know who you are—the Holy One of God!" (Mark 1:24), Jesus sternly commanded the demon, "Be quiet!" (v. 25). The apostle Paul makes it clear that although Jesus was by nature in the form of God, He did not consider equality with God as something to be held onto. Our Lord therefore "emptied Himself" (NAS) (Greek, *eauton ekenosen*) of that quality by which deity would be recognized by men (Phil. 2:6–7). His deity was therefore veiled in human flesh.

No one seeing Jesus thought there was anything unusual about His appearance. There was "nothing in his appearance that we should desire him" (Isa. 53:2). Why do you suppose Judas Iscariot betrayed Jesus with a kiss? (See Matt. 26:48). It was because the chief priests didn't even know what Jesus looked like, but it also shows that there was nothing extraordinary about His appearance.

Paul's main point in the sublime passage in Philippians 2:5–11 was that Jesus refused to vindicate Himself while He was on the earth. He came in the form of a servant and constantly humbled Himself. It was His deity that Jesus in fact kept hidden. All He said to His critics that in fact asserted His deity (John 8:58; 10:30) was not done in order to vindicate Himself so they would back off in their objections, but that all men might see it was the truth about *God* to which they objected.

And yet all these things Jesus said about Himself shows He

was personally conscious of His deity. His critics also could see that the things He said about Himself could add up to only one thing: the claim to deity. But did they believe it? Not for a moment. Neither was Jesus trying to get them to believe it. What He said about Himself would be believed only by the Holy Spirit. What is made clear by the Spirit is most offensive otherwise.

But when Jesus had this conversation with Martha, He was wanting to show her His glory. Whereas Jesus did this with Peter, James, and John by being transfigured before them (Matt. 17:2), with Martha, Jesus was doing it only by His Word. Thus when He said, "I am the resurrection and the life..." (John 11:25), He claimed to be the very cause that would lie behind men and women being raised at the last day. It was a claim to deity that Jesus clearly wanted Martha to grasp. That God Almighty alone could raise Lazarus on the last day went without saying. But the assertion "I am the resurrection and the life..." brought, as it were, the last day to now. Martha was in the very presence of God.

THE MOST HIDDEN TRUTH

This is not all. By saying, "I am the resurrection and the life..." He claimed all life that comes by the Holy Spirit is *Jesus's* own work! It is the essential work of Jesus Christ that the Holy Spirit shows men and women who He is. This is why Jesus claimed to be the resurrection *and the life*. Why did He add "life"? It is because Christ alone authorizes the Holy Spirit to give life. This is why Jesus could say to the Father that the Son would give eternal life (John 17:2).

The word *life* includes regeneration. This means being "born again." When Jesus said to Nicodemus, "You must be born again" (John 3:7), He was speaking of spiritual life, or regeneration. The first birth is natural, or physical. The second birth is supernatural, that is, spiritual. It is when the part of you that has been "dead" because of sin has been quickened (Eph. 2:1). Jesus said, "The Spirit gives life; the flesh counts for nothing" (John 6:63).

But in the claim to be the resurrection and the life, Jesus asserted His deity not only with reference to giving men physical life but also spiritual life. "For just as the Father raises the dead and gives them life, even so the Son gives life to whom he is pleased to give it" (John 5:21). "No one knows the Father except the Son and those to whom the Son chooses to reveal him" (Matt. 11:27). Thus, all that Jesus was now taking the time to say to Martha disclosed that He was God indeed.

Why should Jesus take the time to reveal His deity to one woman whose testimony would do little for His reputation but pass by the chief priests and learned scholars in Jerusalem? I don't know. But that is in fact what happened. The nearest we may ever come to answering this question is by Jesus Himself: "Lord of heaven and earth, because you have hidden these things from the wise and learned, and revealed them to little children. Yes, Father, for this was your good pleasure" (Matt. 11:25–26).

It should be seen, therefore, that although the deity of Jesus Christ is the most fundamental belief of the Christian faith, it is equally the most hidden truth. It is impossible to believe it except by the Holy Spirit. And then when it is seen how this glorious truth passes by so many, and yet you and I see it, we can but fall on our faces and thank God for His mercy by His stooping to where we are and letting us see this truth. I will admit to you that I have no idea why God would reveal to me that Jesus is God. I see it clearly. But this is only because the Holy Spirit enabled me to see it. I can take no credit for it. I never shall be able to take credit for it. All I can do is worship.

If you should be reading these lines but have not as yet been persuaded of all we have been saying, may I suggest that you follow carefully the words of the hymn writer:

> Pass me not, O gentle Savior,
> Hear my humble cry;
> While on others Thou art calling,
> Do not pass me by.[2]
> —Fanny Jane Crosby

If a person is born again, then it is solely the consequence of our Lord Jesus Christ authorizing the Holy Spirit to do it.

Whoever Lives and Believes in Me

There is still more to be seen in Jesus's marvelous words to Martha. Jesus was saying here that all faith is to be directed to Him. "He who *believes in me* will live, even though he dies; and whoever lives and believes in *me* will never die" (John 11:25–26, emphasis added). To direct one's faith to Himself as Jesus did either means that Jesus was a deceiver, a lunatic, or God. No person would ever talk like this to another human being unless He was an utter phony, a madman, or very God. Who else could look into the eyes of a person and say, "He who lives and believes in me will never die"? Jesus was actually asking Martha to put all her trust in one person—Him.

And yet this is the way Jesus spoke all the time. "Come to me, all you who are weary and burdened, and I will give you rest. Take my yoke upon you and learn from me, for I am gentle and humble in heart, and you will find rest for your souls" (Matt. 11:28–29). Jesus later said, "I am the way and the truth and the life. No one comes to the Father except through me" (John 14:6).

Should a Muslim be reading these lines, may I gently say to you that the greatest thing that can ever happen to you is to see that Jesus was God in the flesh. You have believed in Allah. The word *Allah* simply means God. Jesus said, "Ye believe in God, believe also in me" (John 14:1, KJV). If you are a Muslim, Jesus invites you to see who He is. He calls you now—through this very book. It is for you.

And yet this would be true if you are a Hindu, a Sikh, a Buddhist, or one who has been influenced by a cult, such as a Shintoist or a Jehovah's Witness. May God grant that Satan, "the god of this age," will be defeated in your life and that you will be given grace to see "the light of the gospel of the glory of Christ, who is the image of God" (2 Cor. 4:4). It will mean that Jesus Himself has come directly to you by authorizing the Holy Spirit to dispel the blindness of your spiritual eyes. May God grant that this very thing is happening now.

This needs to happen to you, even if you are outwardly a very moral person. It could be that you have kept yourself from sexual immorality, from being a thief and liar, and from doing a lot of the things that others do. If you have kept yourself from wickedness, you may feel offended that you will not be granted entrance into the kingdom of God by your good works. I do understand. But this is why the gospel is so offensive. Christ died for sinners (Rom. 5:8). It may seem a shame that a wicked sinner would be given light to see the glory of Christ while you, a righteous person, would be sent to hell. But I can tell you why. Self-righteousness is as awful in the sight of God as any other wickedness. Self-righteousness is sin (1 John 1:8, 10). Our righteousness is as "filthy rags" in God's sight (Isa. 64:6).

What a pity if you should trust your good works and die in that condition! It need not happen! Don't you see that your heart too needs to be cleansed? You too need to be born again or you will not see the kingdom of God (John 3:3). This is why Jesus said to self-righteous people, "Prostitutes are entering the kingdom of God ahead of you" (Matt. 21:31).

In these lines to Martha, Jesus made it clear that people must see the truth while they are still alive. "Whoever *lives* and believes in me will never die" (John 11:26, emphasis added). Faith is only possible while you are still alive. You will, of course, see who Jesus is eventually. Jesus knew that the day would come when all men would see the very truth He was now privately sharing with Martha. But for the record, Jesus inserted the words, "Whoever lives and believes in me," clarifying that one must see this while one is living.

THERE IS TIME

You are alive, aren't you? This means there is time—at least you have opportunity now. All of us are going to die. I realize that this is not a pleasant subject. But I do you no favor not to remind you that you, like myself, will pass through death's chilly waters. A day will come when we shall realize that "our time is up." How kind of Jesus to insert a warning in His statement to Martha, "Whoever lives and believes in me," lest it be thought that seeing this about Jesus later would be soon enough. No. "Now is the day of salvation" (2 Cor. 6:2). "Today, if you hear his voice, do not harden your hearts" (Heb. 3:7–8).

Jesus promised, moreover, that confessing Him in faith now exempts a person from everlasting hell. This is what He meant by the words "will never die." He did not mean that faith in Him exempts us from going through the crisis of physical death. He had just said, "He who believes in me will live, even though he dies" (John 11:25). In other words, Jesus acknowledged in the same phrase that we are going to die. "Man is destined to die once" (Heb 9:27). This is because "the wages of sin is death" (Rom. 6:23). We *all* must receive our wages for sinning. This means death. We all will receive the wages of sin by dying, even though we have trusted in the merits of Jesus Christ. Jesus therefore stipulated that we would still die even though we trust Him. But what about hell? Answer: "Whoever lives and believes in me will never die" (John 11:26).

But what about hell? Eternal punishment is called "the second death" (Rev. 20:14). The first death is our physical death. The second death is the punishment due to those who die without having put their personal trust in Christ. To put it another way, the second death is meted out to those who ratify their own condemnation. To ratify means to confirm or give validity to. All of us are born into condemnation. Jesus said, "Whoever believes in him [that is, Himself] is not condemned, but whoever does not believe stands condemned already because he has not believed in the name of God's one and only Son" (John 3:18). Hearing the gospel is not what condemns a person, even if he doesn't believe it. Jesus says he is condemned anyway. He "stands condemned already." This is because all men are born condemned. "This is the verdict: Light has come into the world, but men loved darkness instead of light because their deeds were evil" (John 3:19). But those who do not come to the light for fear of their deeds being exposed (John 3:20) thus give validity to the condemnation to which they were born. God said they were condemned; their lives prove it.

To put it yet another way, the difference between the Christian and the non-Christian is this: The Christian mocks his condemnation by faith in Christ. The non-Christian ratifies his condemnation by not coming to Christ. Both the Christian and the non-Christian were born into the *same* condemnation. Paul said that even those who are saved "were by nature objects of wrath" (Eph. 2:3). "Whoever believes in the Son has eternal life, but whoever rejects the Son will not see life, for God's wrath remains on him" (John 3:36).

THE SECOND DEATH

To those who ratify their condemnation, then comes "the second death." It is also called "the lake of fire" (Rev. 20:14). Who exactly will be thrown into the lake of fire? John answers: "If anyone's name was not found written in the book of life, he was thrown into the lake of fire" (Rev. 20:15). It is an awful teaching. I take no pleasure whatsoever in sharing this with the reader. I do so because I must. What kind of friend would I be if I knew of impending doom but did not warn you? Would you not agree, if the biblical teaching of eternal punishment is true, then the kindest thing we can do is to warn people about it? Not telling people about it does not diminish its truth or existence.

I fear that there are a lot of people who know what the Bible teaches with regard to eternal punishment but keep hoping that it is not true, that they misunderstood it, or they think that it will make enemies of the church if they talk about it. If men are already enemies of God and the church anyway, where are we going to send them? Do you entice people to love the church by withholding the truth? They will find it out anyway. It is strange, very strange, that we have allowed Satan to sweep this teaching under the carpet with the hope that we can give God a "better image" to the world.

God is not looking for public relations people. He is looking for prophets.

The German philosopher Ludwig Feuerbach, who was to be a dominant influence on Karl Marx, claimed that God is nothing more than man's projection on the backdrop of the universe. He said that man simply wanted to dream of a

"God up there," as it were, One who is perfect and wonderful and who will reward us after a hard life. But if it was all man's projection, I ask, who would ever have come up with Jesus's teaching on hell? Is hell man's projection on the backdrop of the universe? What man would have wished for this? Answer: No man would ever have dreamed of the lake that burns with fire and brimstone. It is beyond man. Only God conceived it because God made it "for the devil and his angels" (Matt. 25:41).

I don't understand it. I don't know why God made hell, even for the devil and his angels. Abraham did not know why God told him to sacrifice his son Isaac, but he obeyed (Gen. 22:1–18). It was Abraham, moreover, who saw Sodom and Gomorrah about to go up in flames (without any warning from God that we know of) and asked, "Will not the Judge of all the earth do right?" (Gen. 18:25). I would urge this stance by all of us. Will not the Judge of all the earth do right? Let us lower our voices; let us put our intellectual sophistication in suspension. God said, "For my thoughts are not your thoughts, neither are your ways my ways.... As the heavens are higher than the earth, so are my ways higher than your ways and my thoughts than your thoughts" (Isa. 55:8–9).

I know this, that believing and confessing Jesus's deity will spare us the second death. "Whoever lives and believes in me will never die" (John 11:26). That is how important Jesus's own teaching is concerning His deity.

Does He care if we acknowledge His deity? Yes. So much so that He took the time to *ask* Martha to confess the same with her mouth. "Do you believe this?" (v. 26).

It was such a humbling thing for Jesus to do. He who was God, but who made Himself "nothing" (Phil. 2:7), would now condescend by gently leading Martha to see what He really was by nature. I cannot imagine the president trying to explain to someone he meets that he is the president, much less asking a person if he or she believes it! But Jesus did.

Jesus wanted Martha to confess Him. He explained who He was and then asked if she believed.

I wish Jesus would ask me that! And yet He did, and does. He comes by the Holy Spirit with His Word and leads us by the hand, gently persuading us that He is God.

Martha told him: "Yes, Lord...I believe that you are the Christ, the Son of God, who was to come into the world" (John 11:27). In affirming Jesus's deity, she was assured of eternal life.

And yet Martha affirmed even more than that. In her confession she revealed what she believed about the Scriptures. She actually affirmed what the Old Testament taught about Jesus: "You are the Christ, the Son of God, *who was to come* into the world" (John 11:27, emphasis added). Her confession showed what she thought of the Bible and how she connected messiahship, the deity of Christ, and His coming into one person and event.

The Old Testament had forecast the coming of Messiah for hundreds of years. Ask anyone who is Jewish. Most Jews rejected Jesus, but not all of them. Are you Jewish? Are you looking for Messiah?

Neither Will You Be Ashamed

When I was in seminary in Louisville, Kentucky, I was given the privilege of writing a major paper on "The Messianic Hope of Modern Israel" in conjunction with a trip to Israel in 1972. I talked to people in Israel generally, and Jerusalem particularly, ranging from prominent rabbis to secular Jews. It was my conclusion that an extremely small percentage of Jews, even in Israel, seriously entertain any hope of Messiah.

Tourists are often misled by the number of Jews who pray at the Wailing Wall. Because most tourists go to the Wailing Wall, and there are always Jews praying there—indeed, many praying for Messiah—many go away thinking that Israel is generally looking forward to Messiah. Not so. Those who are regularly at the Wailing Wall are mostly a certain type of orthodox Jew who represent an extremely small minority in Israel. They merely get the attention.

A great number of Jews today have little or no expectation of the coming of Messiah—some don't even know what the Bible says about Him. It was my privilege, many years ago, to lead a Jewish businessman to the Lord. He was on his way from Los Angeles to Moscow. A friend of his persuaded him to come to Westminster Chapel in England, where I was preaching at the time. The Holy Spirit arrested him on the very night he came!

When our baptistery was refurbished, he was the first I had the privilege of baptizing. He is now in heaven. I tried later to lead members of his family to Christ. But I will never forget what one of them said to me when I pleaded that she at least read the Psalms. She said, "Is that in the Old Testament or

New Testament?" I didn't anticipate her asking such a question. Because she was Jewish, I realized that I fully expected her to be knowledgeable of the Bible.

And yet many Jews are turning to Jesus Christ in ever-increasing numbers. Are you Jewish? Let me lead you by the hand, as Jesus did with Martha, and point you to the One who said, "I am the resurrection and the life. He who believes in me will live, even though he dies; and whoever lives and believes in me will never die. Do you believe this?" (John 11:25–26).

Do you? Your life will be transformed. Neither will you be ashamed.

My Jewish friend, whom I just referred to, used to arrange for me to be seated at center court every year at Wimbledon to observe the championship tennis matches held there. He happened to know many important people and almost all the players. One by one he introduced me to them as being "the man who changed my life."

But it certainly wasn't me! That is what Jesus did. He will do it for you too. He will change your life. It is called being "born again." Isn't that a lovely phrase? It can happen to you.

8

DOES JESUS CARE
WHEN WE CRY?

Most of us put off crying as long as possible. It is painful to cry when we are alone, and more so in front of someone. I almost think I'd rather die than to be seen when I cry.

But there comes a time when there is nothing else to do. And yet, like being ill, we almost always feel better afterward. Crying gives a certain inner release from tension.

Most of us are probably more like either Martha or Mary. I myself am more like Martha. I am not sure why, but I have suspected that my being more "cerebral" than "emotional" by temperament was owing partly to a reaction against the emotional atmosphere of my old church in Ashland, Kentucky. As far back as I can remember, there was a revival atmosphere in my old church. It seemed to spawn an awful lot of weeping and even shouting. It was not at all uncommon to see grown men and women weeping openly in the services, some of whom made their way to the aisles and did nothing but walk with their arms waving in the air. They were happy people, but I myself didn't particularly like it at the time. Once, when I was six years old, I ran out of the church during the service, and my father found me outside.

"What's wrong?" he asked.

"I don't like all that noise," I answered.

And yet, all of us are emotional creatures, even those who have the strongest "stiff upper lip"! I have discovered one thing about the stiff upper lip—which I have not yet cultivated—and that is it is sometimes a cover for a very deep feeling of emotion inside. When I lived in England, I found that the British are indeed emotional people, but they don't like to show it. In this I am the same, but I have not been as successful in hiding it.

Does Jesus care when we cry? In this chapter we will look more at Mary than Martha. You may recall that Mary was the more emotional of the two, and probably the younger sister. Sibling rivalry has a way of producing opposites, although it is done quite unconsciously. If the older child is intellectual, the younger will often be more emotional. If the older is melancholy, the younger will tend to be more cheerful. If the older is more conscientious and responsible, the younger will often be more playful. If the older is a bit of a workaholic, the younger will probably be more easygoing.

SOME EXPRESS WHAT OTHERS FEEL

Both Martha and Mary, however, felt the same about Jesus not arriving until four days after Lazarus's funeral. Both came to the same conclusion, whether arriving at the decision via intellectual calculation or gut-level instinct.

But from then on, their differences in temperament clearly emerged. Martha began to express her faith, and Mary her feelings of sorrow. When Mary saw Jesus, she fell at His feet and cried her heart out.

Yet I find Mary somewhat more attractive than I do Martha. For those of us who are more analytical and calculating, there is something terribly refreshing about the person who dares to express his or her feelings. All of us often tend to feel exactly the same thing. But for those who do *express* what the rest *feel*, there is admiration. We get a vicarious satisfaction from seeing someone who dares to be less inhibited.

One of the deacons in a church where I formerly ministered once commented on those within the congregation who sometimes worshiped by raising a hand in the air. He told me that he would never be found doing such a thing, "but I am glad when I see others do it." I thought that was quite candid; it points to the way many of us feel. The Marys of this world give spice to life.

Both Martha and Mary received word that Jesus was walking down the road toward their house. Martha got up and went out to meet Him, "but Mary stayed at home" (John 11:20). Both made a deliberate choice. And yet both wanted to get Jesus's attention. Martha managed by expressing her faith in Jesus's power, Mary by her crying.

Mind you, crying can be a manipulative thing. In Everett Shostrom's book *Man, the Manipulator*, he shows that there are essentially two kinds of manipulator—active and passive.[1] We are all manipulators. We tend, at times, to treat people as objects in order to achieve a certain result. The active, overt manipulator is more obvious, the passive less so. But weeping, like Mary, could have been a manipulative device to get Jesus's attention.

We have all done this. Mordecai, in order to get Queen Esther's attention, "...put on sackcloth and ashes, and went out into the city, wailing loudly and bitterly" (Esth. 4:1). When Arthur Blessitt was put out of "His Place," the name he gave his coffeehouse in Hollywood's Sunset Spring, he took down the large wooden cross he had erected against the wall, chained himself to it outside on the sidewalk, and started a fast. A wife may have to go to certain lengths to get her husband's attention when she feels neglected. Her husband at the office may be under pressure to get recognition for his latest idea. Manipulation need not be a bad thing, but perhaps we should realize that this is what we are doing when we are trying to secure a certain effect.

It may sound contradictory, but I believe that God Himself often brings us to tears in order to break us, but also that we might, in turn, move His heart. It is like asking the question, which comes first: the chicken or the egg? Tears touch God's heart, and yet it is His secret providence that lies behind our very coming to tears.

Mary was very hurt. She sat at Jesus's feet when He came to their house for dinner. Martha was annoyed that Mary didn't help to get things ready. Jesus rebuked Martha and approved of Mary (Luke 10:41–42). Mary had listened with deepest interest to what Jesus said. He knew how much she respected Him and His teachings. Both sisters thought it not unreasonable to send word to Jesus that their brother, Lazarus, was unwell. But Lazarus died and was buried. After four days, here came Jesus. Martha went out to meet Jesus; Mary stayed behind as the tears began to flow.

Tears: Happy and Sad

There are, of course, happy causes for tears. Tears can come from a feeling of joy. A preacher can make a good point in a sermon and bring his congregation to tears. It can happen to us when we are watching a moving scene on television.

One of the few times in my life that I have wept openly for joy was when a particular man whom many had been praying for came to my church in Fort Lauderdale and was gloriously converted.

We were conscious of his presence in the service. That in itself was an answer to prayer. He had been hostile to the church and the gospel. But, unexpectedly, this man for whom the congregation had been praying attended a church service and was seated halfway back next to the aisle. God gave me unusual power in the sermon. When we gave the invitation for people to come forward, I saw that he was under conviction, even quite unable to sing the hymn "Just as I Am." He gripped the pew in front of him so hard that I thought his blood vessels would burst! But then he came, almost staggering down the aisle as his shoulders shook from his sobbing. I left the pulpit, welcomed and embraced him, and wept openly on his shoulders. There wasn't a dry eye in the place.

But Mary's crying was not for joy. Her crying was a result of three things—hurt, sorrow, and dismay. The hurt was due to her bitterness that Jesus had not come at first. The sorrow was what anyone would feel when a loved one dies. But the dismay she felt was owing to the realization, or so it seemed, that the outlook was sheer bleakness. There was no hope. It was too late. Why should He come now?

Although Mary did not go out of the house with her sister to meet Jesus, she did go shortly afterward. After Martha and Jesus had finished their wonderful conversation, Martha went back to the house and called Mary to one side: "'The Teacher is here,' she said, 'and is asking for you'" (John 11:28).

Despite the bitterness that Mary felt, I suspect she was in fact overjoyed that Jesus sent for her. Often our sulking does not exhibit the *whole* of our feelings. We can feel bitter but hope nonetheless that the one against whom we feel bitter will beckon us. This is what happened.

What an honor it was to get a personal invitation like that from Jesus. Can anything in this world be greater than to have the Lord Jesus Christ in the flesh bother to send for someone? More than anything I can imagine, I would rather have a word from Him in which He asks me to come to Him. Few people in the New Testament were singled out by Jesus in this manner. Peter and Andrew received a personal call, as did James and John (Matt. 4:18–22). Zacchaeus got attention like that (Luke 19:5).

And yet all those whom Jesus calls, He calls in a personal, individual manner. As God loves every man as though there were no one else to love, so He calls each man individually, personally, particularly, and so definitely that the person being called is aware of God's love as though there were no one else.

GET UP QUICKLY

Whatever hurt Mary was feeling, it was sweet relief when she heard the moving invitation via Martha. There was no question or hesitation about what Mary would do with this invitation. "When Mary heard this, she got up quickly and went to him" (John 11:29).

Are you feeling a bit like Mary at the moment? Do you feel let down by the Lord? Do you feel that He has neglected you? Perhaps you have not gone to church lately while others, who may have similar thoughts to you, go nonetheless to meet with the Lord. They go to church and enjoy fellowship with Him and His people. But you, like Mary, stay at home. Are you really better off?

What you want to hear more than anything in the world is a definite word from the Lord. You are hurt, yes. But you would be in despair if the Lord reacted to your hurt on the same level as you have reacted to His delay in answering your prayer. One of you has to be the "bigger," the more magnanimous. You are hoping in your heart of hearts that the Lord will overlook your bitterness and send word that He is asking for you.

He is. He comes now. The Teacher is here and is asking for you. He loves you. He knows you. A true friend is someone who knows all about you and still likes you! Jesus knew

Mary backward and forward. He knows you too. He understands. As the psalmist put it, "For he knoweth our frame; he remembereth that we are dust" (Ps. 103:14, KJV). He is sending for you. Go now; go out to meet Him. He sends for you, knowing *exactly* what you are going to say, and He is prepared to listen.

Do it as Mary did. Get up quickly! Do not delay! The devil will slip in and tell you that Jesus does not care. When the Lord calls, you must act "today, if you hear his voice" (Heb. 3:7). Do not quench the Spirit: "Do not put out the Spirit's fire" (1 Thess. 5:19).

The Lord calls us, knowing exactly how we feel. He knows we feel justified for our hurt. But He is not threatened by that. He comes anyway. He is prepared to "take it" from us as though we have a right to feel as we do. The Lord found Jonah in this condition immediately after Nineveh repented. Jonah should have been happy, but he wasn't. He had no right to be angry, but he thought he did. The Lord did not scold or lecture Him. "Then said the LORD, Doest thou well to be angry?" (Jon. 4:4, KJV). It was as though the Lord put His arms around Jonah and said, "You are angry, aren't you?"

The Lord is touched with the feeling of our weaknesses (Heb. 4:15). This does not mean that we are right to feel as we do or that He is approving of how we feel. He just comes and says, "You are hurt, aren't you?"

THE WILL OF THE FATHER

When Jesus originally received the signal from the Father to stay behind rather than go and heal Lazarus straightaway,

He knew then how Martha and Mary would feel. Devoted to Lazarus's sisters though He was, His devotion to the Father had priority. "For even Christ did not please himself" (Rom. 15:3). "'My food,' said Jesus, 'is to do the will of him who sent me'" (John 4:34). The Son "…can do only what he sees his Father doing, because whatever the Father does the Son also does" (John 5:19). Part of our Lord's suffering was knowing how men would react to the hard decisions He had to make again and again—all because He came not to do His own will but the will of "…him who sent me" (John 5:30).

We too are called to be like Jesus. We too have to make decisions that will often displease those closest to us. It is part of bearing the cross that we take our orders from above.

And yet how wonderful it is that the same loving Father who ordered His Son not to go and heal Lazarus also told Him to send for Mary. This action too was the consequence of Jesus's seeing what the Father wanted Him to do. Our Lord reflects the love of the Father in all that He does, all that He permits, all that He allows to happen that He very well knows will not make us happy at first.

But as Jesus now gave priority to accepting Mary in her grief, we may constantly keep in mind that this too was simultaneously the Father's will. Never think that there is any disparity between Jesus and the Father. All that Jesus was and is mirrors the Father. "Anyone who has seen me has seen the Father" (John 14:9).

I have heard people claim to like Jesus but not God the Father, as though there was a difference of opinion between the two. Such a person ought to keep in mind that what he *does* like about Jesus was *also* our Lord carrying out the Father's will. It was therefore the Father whom he actually liked when he thought he was liking Jesus.

Jesus was now prepared to "take it" from Mary. He wasn't particularly looking forward to the moment when she would fall at his feet and accuse Him of all her sadness. But when God took the decision to eternity to become man, He fully calculated the man situation. This is why Jesus was depicted as a "man of sorrows" (Isa. 53:3). He came to the earth with very big shoulders. He lets us cry on them, knowing full well that we often blame Him for our suffering.

CALLED ASIDE—MARY'S MOMENT CAME

Martha did something that was very discreet. After her conversation with Jesus, she went back to the house "and called her sister Mary aside" (John 11:28). She called her "secretly" (KJV). Why secretly? Why call Mary aside? Because Martha saw no need for all the friends and neighbors to witness Mary's emotional outburst. Martha suggested that Mary come out alone and see Jesus a good distance from the house and "have her say" with Him in private. Why let the world witness a family quarrel?

Martha shrewdly hoped to protect Mary from those who did not need to know all that was in Mary's heart. There is no need for the world to know all the thoughts of those in the church. The church is a very mixed people. They come from all walks of life and have ailments, hurts, problems, questions, divisions, and dilemmas that need not be broadcast to the world.

Only sadder than the disunity of the body of Christ are those who seem more anxious to tell the world what our internal differences are than they are to convert the world. But Martha was not like that. She called Mary "aside."

It is Satan who wants the church to hang all its dirty linen out for the world to enjoy. I suspect that when we have a greater love for God's kingdom, we will begin to want to see people saved more than we want to get individual vindication for the smaller points that tend to divide sincere Christians. But we have all done this. There are few Marthas around.

Mary's moment came. She probably had rehearsed it a hundred times over the previous four days. She knew that Jesus would eventually arrive. "She fell at his feet and said, 'Lord, if you had been here, my brother would not have died'" (John 11:32).

It was a painful moment for Mary. There was a manipulative element present, yes, but her hurt was real. The tears were real. Her dilemma was real. It made no sense to her whatsoever that the Lord would come to see her four days after the funeral, when He could have come so easily while Lazarus was still alive—to heal him.

Yet what a wonderful thing it is to be able to cry. Tears can be medicinal. As sweat pours from our bodies to keep us cool on a hot day, so do tears pour from our eyes to keep our souls from falling apart. God grants to all of us the privilege of crying when we are hurt, lonely, dismayed, under pressure, and feeling that there is absolutely no hope left. Tears are God's own gift for such a time as this. He shows us that He cares by inviting us to cry.

In my pastoral experience, I have watched people who were in agony but unable to shed a tear. I have seen them want to cry, but they couldn't. There have been a few occasions when I actually encouraged them to cry. When I succeeded they *always* felt better. I saw one person who finally let himself go. When he began to sob, his shoulders shook, his voice trembled, and his emotional display was almost frightening. But after about ten minutes, he looked at me and simply said, "Thanks."

Despite Martha's plan that Mary should come out and see the Lord privately, Mary's Jewish neighbors followed her, thinking only that she was going to the tomb (John 11:31). Whether she managed to unburden her heart to Jesus before the rest arrived, I don't know. Sometimes it is inevitable that others look in on a private matter that one hopes will remain private. In any case, it did not stop the Lord from doing what He intended to do in the end.

A Time for Weeping

Does Jesus care when we weep? Yes. He notices: "Jesus saw her weeping" (John 11:33). That alone probably did Mary more good than anything else. Hagar said, "You are the God who sees me" (Gen. 16:13). When I call to mind that my God sees and knows what is happening I take great courage.

Jesus responds to each of us according to our need, our temperament, and our personalities. Martha, seeming less emotional and more intellectual, was able, in her grief, to talk theology! So Jesus continued with her at that level.

There are some who get their comfort by an intellectual breakthrough, a theological clarification. Others are not able to think along abstract lines with only the heart. Such was Mary: her heart ached. Jesus responded to her in kind: "When Jesus saw her weeping, and the Jews who had come along with her also weeping, he was deeply moved in spirit and troubled" (John 11:33).

In my old church in Kentucky, they used to sing the following little chorus every week, just before prayer time:

> Standing somewhere in the shadows you'll find Jesus,
> He's the only One who cares and understands;
> Standing somewhere in the shadows you will find Him,
> And you'll know Him by the nail prints in his hand.[2]
> —E. J. ROLLINGS

Our Lord meets us at our level. He can relate to the most sophisticated intellectual; He can make the simplest mind feel at home—and important—in His presence. There is "a time to weep and a time to laugh..." (Eccles. 3:4). The greatest Pastor who ever was knows how to rejoice with those who are rejoicing and to weep with those who are weeping (Rom. 12:15).

He does not laugh at us when we are crying. He does not make us feel guilty. He never moralizes. Never does He make us feel ashamed when He finds us weeping.

It may be that bringing us to tears is part of God's plan. Could it be that God wanted to bring Mary to tears before He would do anything extraordinary? Could it be that this is why Jesus had to wait behind and not appear until four days after the funeral? "Those who sow in tears will reap with songs of joy. He who goes out weeping, carrying seed to sow, will return with songs of joy, carrying sheaves with him" (Ps. 126:5–6).

In 1956 I read an article by Maynard James titled "Try Tears." His point was that the church tries everything else. We have tried organization, new methods, new ways, and new faces in order to bring down God's blessing on us. "Let's try tears," said Maynard James.

I developed a sermon on tears that I preached in the Soviet Union. I will never forget preaching it in Latvia and the response it got. As we were walking into the service, Sergei Nikolaev whispered to me, "What are you going to preach on?"

"Tears," I answered. He looked puzzled and shrugged his shoulders, wondering what was to follow. But the Holy Spirit came on the service powerfully, and many said I had the exact word that was needed. People wept all over the house.

TEARS MOVE THE HEART OF GOD

Do you want to get God's attention? Try tears. Why? Because tears are one thing God cannot stand to watch for very long. It is a strain that runs right through the Bible. Nothing moves the heart of God like tears. It is as though the one thing He cannot bear is our tears.

The first time the word *tears* can be found in the King James Version of the Bible is in 2 Kings 20:5: "... I have heard your prayer and seen your tears." This was God's response to Hezekiah after he wept before the Lord when he heard the news that he would die. God told Hezekiah to set his house in order "...because you are going to die; you will not recover" (v. 1) from the illness that beset him. Hezekiah did not take the news gladly. He "turned his face to the wall" and "wept bitterly" (vv. 2–3). God came to Hezekiah a second time and promised healing after all, that Hezekiah would in fact live another fifteen years: "I have heard your prayer and seen your tears" (v. 5). I myself do not take too seriously what some Bible scholars call "the law of the first mention," when the meaning accompanying a particular word the first time it appears will retain that meaning essentially throughout the Bible. But I am tempted to go along with the idea of the law of first mention in this case. For tears moved God's heart—so much so that God appeared to change His mind.

The repeated references to tears in the psalms indicate that God takes very serious notice of our weeping. "I am worn out from groaning; all night long I flood my bed with weeping and drench my couch with tears" (Ps. 6:6). "Hear my prayer, O LORD, listen to my cry for help; be not deaf to my weeping" (Ps. 39:12). "My tears have been my food day and night, while men say to me all day long, 'Where is your God?'" (Ps. 42:3). "Record my lament; list my tears on your scroll—are they not in your record?" (Ps. 56:8).

One day Jesus happened to notice a funeral procession. It turned out that a widow was following the coffin in which her only son lay. That was more than Jesus could take. "When the Lord saw her, his heart went out to her and he said, 'Don't cry.' Then he went up and touched the coffin, and those carrying it stood still. He said, 'Young man, I say to you, get up!' The dead man sat up and began to talk, and Jesus gave him back to his mother" (Luke 7:13–15).

Tears move God's heart. If you are brought to tears, be encouraged. You are getting God's attention.

Tears reflect a humble state that God also wants to see in us. "For everyone who exalts himself will be humbled, and he who humbles himself will be exalted" (Luke 14:11). "God opposes the proud but gives grace to the humble" (James 4:6). "Humble yourselves, therefore, under God's mighty hand, that he may lift you up in due time" (1 Pet. 5:6). Tears may be evidence that a real humbling process has taken place in our hearts. This may be why God says, "Those who sow in tears will reap with songs of joy" (Ps. 126:5).

Part of the greatness of the apostle Paul lay perhaps in his candor about tears. Paul made a farewell speech to the elders of the church at Ephesus and said, "I served the Lord with great humility and with tears...Remember that for three years I never stopped warning each of you night and day with tears" (Acts 20:19, 31). Paul reminded the Corinthians, "I wrote you out of great distress and anguish of heart and with many tears, not to grieve you but to let you know the depth of my love for you" (2 Cor. 2:4). And Paul commented to Timothy that he remembered his tears (2 Tim. 1:4).

One of the most pathetic cases of demon possession in the New Testament was that of a boy who from childhood would convulse, foam at the mouth, and be thrown into fire. The boy's father pleaded with Jesus to bring relief. Jesus said to him, "All things are possible to him that believeth. And straightway the father of the child cried out, *and said with tears*, Lord, I believe; help thou mine unbelief!" (Mark 9:23–24, KJV, emphasis added). Jesus then cast the demon out of the young man.

Try tears. God takes notice of tears. You will find that God is on the side of the oppressed. He is for the poor. He is on the side of the one who is rejected by society. He is for the one who has been the object of racial prejudice. He is on the side of the widow. He aches for that single parent who must bring up children on a very meager income.

Are you wanting to overcome a particular habit? It may be a drinking problem or a sexual problem; try tears. Do you have a cultural problem, an illness, financial pressure? Do you have difficulties with someone at work or with your own personality? Is it loneliness, fear of having to remain single, sorrow over the loss of someone very close to you? Is it being passed over for the job you wanted, being turned down after sending in your application, or being misunderstood by one who ought to have known the situation? Are you involved with a church without God's obvious blessing? Try tears. Tears get God's attention.

He Reaches Out and Helps Us Through

Perhaps you feel a sense of shame over what has recently happened. You have let down yourself, your parents, your husband or wife, or your children. You have contemplated ending it all because you have nothing more to live for. Try tears. Jesus will notice, "A bruised reed he will not break" (Matt. 12:20). Jesus loves to reach those who are down.

A few weeks after my mother's death, I found myself in greater sorrow than I had actually known on the day of her death or the day of the funeral. It was weeks later that it all really hit me—my mother was absolutely and irrevocably gone. Gone. She would not be back. I thought that I would die. Kneeling in my old rocking chair, sobbing my heart out, I thought I could not go on. But something strange happened. I still don't understand it. Suddenly it was as though I could actually hear my mother and father singing—a song they used to sing as a duet:

> He's our help in time of trouble,
> He's our best and dearest Friend;
> When I falter, then He whispers,
> "Child, be true."
>
> Though earth's trials may seem many,
> Still on Him I can depend;
> Jesus reaches out His hand,
> And helps us through.[3]
>
> —FLOYD W. HAWKINS

A bruised reed He will not break. Satan loves to kick a man when he is down. The devil is ruthless, evil, and loathes us with an icy hatred that is horrifying. Jesus is the opposite of the devil. He reaches down His hand and helps us through.

Are you humbled because of sin? "It is not the healthy who need a doctor, but the sick. I have not come to call the righteous, but sinners to repentance" (Luke 5:31–32).

JESUS WEPT...SEE HOW HE LOVED

Does Jesus care when we cry? Yes. He cares. He shows it. I bring the reader by the hand now to witness one of the most incredible verses in the Bible. It is in one sense beyond understanding, if only because the Lord Jesus Christ, who had a plan all along, knew how things would shortly turn out. But He became so utterly involved in Mary's weeping, even with the others standing by who wept, that He too followed them. Their tears were too much for Him. It is the shortest verse in the Bible: "Jesus wept" (John 11:35).

Jesus weeps with us when we cry. That is how much He cares. Tears beget tears. When you see another crying, it can be quite contagious. When Jesus saw Mary's distraught spirit, her body having fallen at His feet, He felt only one thing: compassion.

Jesus, of course, knew that Mary did not know what He knew—that He was going to raise Lazarus from the dead in a few minutes' time. He also knew that they would not complain once they discovered that there was a deliberate strategy in His not answering the call to come and heal Lazarus. He knew that they could not see beyond the moment. He entered into their suffering. He was into their skin as though He totally agreed with all their complaints, all their misery, all their hurt. Who would have thought that the Son of God, Maker of heaven and Earth, would enter into the human situation of Martha and Mary as Jesus did—and join them in their crying?

Jesus was "...deeply moved in spirit and troubled" (John 11:33). What caused that feeling? He reacted to them.

God reacts to what He sees in us. And when it is *tears* that He sees, we may know that He is deeply moved. Jesus proves that.

What do you suppose was the reaction of those who witnessed Jesus's weeping? "The Jews said, 'See how he loved him!'" (John 11:36). I should have thought they would say, "See how he loved *them*"—meaning Martha and Mary. But no, they took it to mean that Jesus loved Lazarus.

And Jesus did love Lazarus. That is the way the story began. "Lord, the one you love is sick" (John 11:3). Martha and Mary were right then. And the Jews were right later: "Behold how he loved him!" (John 11:36, KJV). We may have thought that the only ones our Lord cared about were Mary and Martha. But now we can see that Jesus missed Lazarus too. Let no one think that Jesus was happy about letting Lazarus die!

When Martha and Mary put their feelings before Jesus, "Lord, if you had been here, [our] brother would not have died," they were thinking of themselves and virtually accusing Jesus of not caring for them or Lazarus. While He was having to console *them* and understand *them,* it seems not to have entered their minds that Jesus too was grieving for Lazarus. But who would sympathize with Jesus? He also lost a friend, but all were thinking of themselves.

God has feelings too. We all want to lean on His big shoulders in our time of grief, but He too feels things that He does not share. Yet, in the end, all will see into His heart.

When the Jews said, "See how he loved him!" it was tantamount to a vindication for the Lord already. For the accusation was: Jesus did not care. It seems to have taken those outside the immediate family of Lazarus, Martha, and Mary to point out how much the Lord cared. They could see that it was Lazarus, as well as Martha and Mary, whom Jesus was weeping for. The world that charges God with not caring will someday see *how much* He really cares. Then the world will weep and wail and gnash their teeth.

Incidentally, the last time the word *tears* appears in the Bible is when John begins to describe the New Jerusalem. God's special name for the place of our inheritance after this present world is dissolved. John said, "He will wipe every tear from their eyes" (Rev. 21:4). What a sight that is going to be when God Himself wipes away the tears from each of our eyes.

What pleasure it will give us—and Him!

9

DOES JESUS CARE WHEN WE ARGUE WITH HIM?

W hen I was a pastor at Westminster Chapel in London and first made the decision to begin the Pilot Light ministry, my wife, Louise, was not over the moon about it. She privately feared that witnessing on the streets was all right for some people (Arthur Blessitt, for example), but not for all—and certainly not for her. But she also felt a little this way about the use of Evangelism Explosion (an evangelism and discipleship training program) in the Chapel. She was not against it, but she did not feel that she herself needed an extended course in how to lead a soul to Jesus Christ. After all, she said, having sat under my ministry for some twenty-five years, she was surely equipped in the knowledge of how to become a Christian.

To my surprise, however, she volunteered to join us one Saturday morning on the streets of Westminster. "Fine," I said, "if that is what you want to do." I never once pressed her to go out on the streets with me. So far as I can recall, I never even suggested it to her. I knew how she felt. Besides, I knew that I had to do it and that it was solely the consequence of the Lord having dealt with me. He could deal with her too.

Apparently she was having her own argument with the Lord during those early weeks in which we did the unprecedented thing—at least for us it hadn't been done before—of walking up to total strangers and asking about their eternal destiny. But she did ask the Lord for some indication that God Himself was in all that we were doing. Perhaps He would give her some sort of sign that the Lord had led me and whether or not she too should be in the streets talking to people about the Lord.

After her second cup of coffee, she walked to St. James's Park tube station (the equivalent of a subway in the States). In the first thirty minutes, she noticed a young man, perhaps aged twenty, wearing a Che Guevara T-shirt. He looked at Louise and walked over to her. With trembling hands and voice she began to offer him my little tract *What Is Christianity?* "I don't suppose you would want one of these, would you?" she asked him. "It is about God and His Son Jesus Christ."

Tears filled the young man's eyes. He looked at her almost in disbelief. "I'm a Marxist," he said. "I'm an atheist. I have never believed in God. But five minutes ago I sat in the pew of a church and said, 'God, if You really exist, let me run into someone who believes in You.'"

He then said to my wife, "I've got to catch a train. But I'll give you five minutes to try to convert me." It was at that point Louise realized she honestly did not know what to say to that young man. She was so ashamed. She tried in desperation to think of the right things, but realized that she too needed a course in soul-winning after all—even after listening to my preaching for twenty-five years! God won the argument. Louise enrolled in the Evangelism Explosion course and was on the streets with us almost every Saturday.

MANY HAVE ARGUED

It is of no small comfort to me to recall that many great men have argued with God—not that this makes God happy! When God told Moses to lead the children of Israel out of Egypt, Moses thought God had surely made a mistake, so "Moses said to the LORD, 'O Lord, I have never been eloquent, neither in the past nor since you have spoken to your servant. I am slow of speech and tongue....O Lord, please send someone else to do it.'" (Exod. 4:10, 13). But Moses was plainly rebuked by God; the anger of the Lord "burned against Moses" (v. 14).

Peter argued with Jesus a number of times. On one occasion Jesus explained to His disciples that He must go to Jerusalem and suffer many things, that He must be killed and be raised to life. Peter took Jesus aside and began to rebuke Him. "'Never, Lord!' he said, 'This shall never happen to you!' Jesus turned and said to Peter, 'Get behind me, Satan! You are a stumbling block to me; you do not have in mind the things of God, but the things of men'" (Matt. 16:22–23).

Later Jesus told Peter one evening, "'This very night, before the rooster crows, you will disown me three times.' But Peter declared, 'Even if I have to die with you, I will never disown you'" (Matt. 26:34–35). But Peter did in fact deny Jesus that very night. After the third time, the rooster crowed, Peter remembered Jesus's words, and "went outside and wept bitterly" (Matt. 26:75).

Even after Peter was restored, filled with the Spirit, and mightily used of God, he argued with Jesus. Once he saw a vision of something "like a large sheet being let down to earth by its four corners. It contained all kinds of four-footed animals, as well as reptiles of the earth and birds of the air. Then a voice told him, 'Get up, Peter. Kill and eat.' 'Surely not, Lord!' Peter replied. 'I have never eaten anything impure or unclean'" (Acts 10:11–14). The voice then rebuked Peter, "Do not call anything impure that God has made clean" (v. 15).

The one thing that all have discovered who argued with God is this: God knew what He was doing when He said what He did, and one finally learns to take God seriously whenever He speaks at all. God never wastes words.

This chapter centers largely on Martha. Perhaps Mary was too overcome with grief and tears to speak. Deeply moved, Jesus walked to Lazarus's tomb. The tomb was in fact a cave with a stone laid across the entrance. Jesus gave a command: "Take away the stone" (John 11:39). It is Martha who blurts out, "But, Lord…by this time there is a bad odor, for he has been there four days" (v. 39).

This aspect of our story shows two different positions that reveal a quarrel with God. One of them is that of Martha: "Lord, by this time there is a bad odor." The other is that of certain observers we examined in chapter 5 who said, "Could not he who opened the eyes of the blind man have kept this man from dying?" (v. 37). The first is arguing *with* God; the latter is arguing *about* God. Those in the family have been known to argue with Him; those outside the family argue about Him.

ARGUING *ABOUT* GOD

Arguing about God is an enterprise in which those outside the family of God are frequently known to engage. They are on the outside looking in. They are quite sure they have a clear grasp of the situation and always feel qualified to speak.

If you are outside the family of God, I might describe you in these terms. Although we haven't met, I know a good deal about you. I should not need your personal history spelled out in order to understand your questions or to know where you are coming from. In saying this I underestimate your own pilgrimage. And yet it is an absolute fact that those outside the family have the same quarrel about God.

In other words, if God can do anything, why doesn't He stop suffering? Arguing about God is always characterized by *assumption*. People tend to assume certain points of view uncritically. People seldom bother to question their assumptions. They seem so right and reasonable at first that one hastily concludes they are self-authenticating proofs for rejecting the existence of God, or that if He does exist, say these people, it proves He doesn't care.

In my conversations with thousands of people on the streets during the past few years, I have discovered a number of things. I have found that *all* men and women have this assumption about God. If they pause to talk for very long with me, I discover that at the bottom of their unbelief is this assumption: the continuation of evil and suffering shows either that God does not exist or that He does not care. This to some is sufficient evidence for safely rejecting Him once and for all. One often senses that some people fancy they are the first to have had this thought! I have perceived many times that people who offer this line really do think it is cleverness that has led them to this conclusion.

But God allowed this question to emerge a long time ago and inserted it right in the middle of our story. The questions, "Could not he who opened the eyes of the blind man have kept this man from dying?" and "Why doesn't an omnipotent God stop evil and suffering?" are exactly the same.

Could it be that your own rationale for not becoming a Christian is that the aforementioned assumption precludes your moving any further toward God with integrity? Perhaps you honestly feel that it would be immoral for you to embrace a God who claims to be holy but allows evil. Your reason, therefore, for rejecting the claims of Jesus Christ is to you a matter of personal integrity. May I ask, has this led you to morality in all *other* areas?

SELF-RIGHTEOUSNESS

I have also learned from witnessing in the streets that all men and women are self-righteous. The proof of this is that when I do succeed in getting them to spend a few minutes, then inquire what hope they have of going to heaven when they die, such hope every time will be in their own efforts. Mind you, when I ask the question, "Do you know for sure that, were you to die today, you would go to heaven?" they often say, "I don't believe in heaven in the first place."

Granted. "But suppose there *were* a heaven," I say to them, "and you did die, and you *did* find yourself standing before God, and He *did* say to you, 'Why should I let you into My heaven?' what *would* you say?" Without exception they betray their own self-righteousness. It does not occur to them that self-righteousness is the essence of sin, and it shows that, regardless of their intelligence, education, culture, or race, they are exactly the way the Bible describes the whole human race. (See Romans 3:23.)

Self-righteousness has a way of masking the more blatant immorality. I can say, without exaggeration, that I have found prostitutes, drug users, convicted criminals, and almost every conceivable type of wickedness to be camouflaged by a feeling of personal righteousness. I have watched them say in apparent innocence, "I have lived a good life." Self-righteousness has a way of blotting out our memories. When we reflect on what we did yesterday, we tend, almost always, to remember what is not unpleasant. Not only that, self-righteousness justifies all that we do—even sin. This is why people can do the most questionable things but never regard them as wrong. Wrong always seems right at first. "There is a way that seems right to a man, but in the end it leads to death" (Prov. 14:12).

ALOOFNESS

Those who argue about God tend to do it from the position of *aloofness*. It is as though they do not want to approach Him directly. Moving to where He actually is, is not regarded as an attractive option, only speaking about Him. Rather than seeking Him, seeking His will, or searching His Word, they remain aloof from Him. To put it another way, they would rather speak to each other *about* God than to address Him directly. They want to keep a certain distance from Him, but not from one another in speaking about Him. Sometimes men would prefer to argue with each other about their own ideas of God than to let God speak for Himself.

Not long ago I happened to walk up to two men who were discussing a position I took in one of my books. When they saw that I was right, they said that they were differing with each other as to what I had taught. "He says you teach this, and I say you teach that," one asserted. I listened to what each of them claimed that I taught, but when I started to quote what I actually said, neither was interested in hearing from me. They preferred instead to debate with each other as to *my* position! They did not want to know what *I said.* I walked away from them as they continued shouting at each other.

Those who said, "Could not he who opened the eyes of the blind man have kept this man from dying?" kept their distance from Jesus. They did not bother to go to Jesus Himself. They wanted instead to talk about Him, to be able to refer to Him. It suggests how insecure such people were and are. They don't want to get so close to the truth that they are personally involved. They want to be able to discuss it from the vantage point of aloofness.

Some people are afraid to seek God through the Bible lest they get converted. This is why some do not go to church. They fear something will happen that will convince them. They much prefer to remain unconverted and be able, nonetheless, to voice their views about God. They find their questioning to one another of the ways of God more attractive than having God Himself to correct them.

It has been reported in recent years that there are fears that the Leaning Tower of Pisa is in danger of falling over. Those in the lovely Italian town who are responsible for this famous tourist sight hired an architect to produce a plan to save it. But they gave this clear instruction: keep the tower from falling, but don't correct the tilt!

We are all like that. We much prefer to live with our imperfections, our doubts, our tendency toward falling; but we don't want to correct our "tilt."

Perhaps you want to remain aloof from the Lord because you have seen the effect He has had on some of your close friends. Have you been surprised to discover who became a Christian? Does this give you a feeling that things are "closing in" on you? Perhaps you have said, "Am I to be next?" Terrified at the prospect of being converted, you remain aloof.

ACCUSATION

Those who wish to argue about God always do so from a position of *accusation*. This was the essential attitude of those who said, "Could not he who opened the eyes of the blind man have kept this man from dying?" (John 11:37). Rather than extol Jesus for opening the eyes of the blind, which they seemed to accept, they wanted to accuse God for what He *didn't* do: keep Lazarus from dying. For people like this, God can do nothing right. Never mind how many wonderful things God has done in the past, we accuse Him for the latest thing He has *not* done.

The children of Israel were like that. No sooner had they been delivered from their terrible bondage in Egypt than they began to complain. Whenever God allowed them to be tested again—which was a splendid opportunity to please Him by faith alone—they would say to Moses, "Was it because there were no graves in Egypt that you brought us to the desert to die?... It would have been better for us to serve the Egyptians than to die in the desert!" (Exod. 14:11–12).

When do you suppose those men who wanted to argue about Jesus letting Lazarus die actually posed the question? It was immediately after Jesus wept. There were two reactions to Jesus's weeping. Certain Jews said, "See how he loved him!" But others said, "Could not he who opened the eyes of the blind man have kept this man from dying?"

Perhaps the latter group of observers was actually moved by the sight of Jesus weeping? They needed a justification for not letting the love of Jesus embrace them. They took refuge in their ability to argue about the Lord by accusation. It was a defense mechanism.

The sight of tears rarely leaves another unaffected. To see Jesus actually weeping at the grave of Lazarus was perhaps too much for some of them to bear. The tears of Jesus left them without excuse.

An old friend of mine, Ernest Reisinger, tells how he was converted. Ernie was once a carpenter in Pennsylvania. A man by the name of Elmer worked with him and faithfully witnessed to him day after day about Jesus Christ. Elmer would invite Ernie to come to his church. Every week Ernie had an excuse. "For a whole year I had fifty-two excuses why I could not be in Elmer's church the following Sunday," says Ernie. But one day Ernest Reisinger finally agreed to go: "All right, Elmer, I will be there on Sunday."

The following Sunday Ernie and his wife drove to Elmer's church. After they got out of their car and walked toward the church, they saw Elmer standing on the steps of the church, waiting for them. When Elmer welcomed his friend that Sunday morning, Ernie says he can only remember one thing. "Tears rolled down his cheeks," says Ernie. "I could never get away from the sight of Elmer's tears."

But tears can produce an opposite reaction too. To some, yes, there will be the response "See how he loved him!" To others there will be a stiff-necked utterance of accusation, "Could not he who opened the eyes of the blind man have kept this man from dying?"

THE LORD'S RESPONSE

It is amazing that some who begin to see the authenticity of the Christian faith retreat into all manner of defenses rather than explore the claims of Jesus Christ. At the tomb of Lazarus, anyone could see how real Jesus was, that He was caring, transparent, hiding nothing. But when some men have sheer authenticity staring them in the face, they still resort to their arguments about God. They betray a lack of real honesty after all.

It will do well for us to see, yet again, what the response of our Lord was to those who accused Him: He said nothing. He was aware of what was being said. He was not unaffected by it, but He did not reply.

The Lord's word to us at this moment is that we shall never know what He is up to until we first remove the stone. However much you may wish to pry into His *secret will* before you obey His *revealed will*, I can tell you that you will never *know* His secret will until you have *obeyed* His revealed will. We shall look at this important distinction.

The Lord was very gracious to Martha. He might have referred to her impertinence in reminding Him of the bad odor that would emerge from the cave. He might also have warned her that she must not argue with His orders. But He didn't. To those in the family there is a most high privilege of being able to share with God what you actually feel without being disfranchised. "As a father has compassion on his children, so the LORD has compassion on those who fear him; for he knows how we are formed, he remembers that we are dust" (Ps. 103:13–14).

The response of Jesus to Martha was merely this: "Did I not tell you that if you believed, you would see the glory of God?" (John 11:40). This is the answer the Lord gives to those in His family who argue with Him. He kindly but firmly points them back to His own Word. But to those outside the family who argue about Him, no answer comes from Him at all. He will answer those outside the family only on the last day.

And yet it was a rebuke to Martha. Don't expect to argue with God without getting a rebuke. As the Lord said to Peter, "What God hath cleansed, *that* call not thou common" (Acts 10:15, KJV). "The Lord disciplines those he loves, and he punishes everyone he accepts as a son" (Heb. 12:6). God's disciplining, or chastening, comes in three stages, although the latter two can be avoided:

1. Internal chastening: when God disciplines by His own Word

2. External chastening: when God's discipline comes from without, as in the case of Jonah's fish

3. Terminal chastening: when God steps in by cutting our lives short because of scandalous sin

Internal chastening is the best way to have our problems dealt with. By taking God's Word to heart, we can be spared the more extreme forms of chastening. It was the first level of chastening that was in operation when the Lord rebuked Martha. "Did I not tell you that if you believed, you would see the glory of God?" (John 11:40).

NOTHING HAS CHANGED

Our Lord always reminds us of His original word to us. Sometimes we fancy that either the Lord did not mean what He said at first or, perhaps, He has forgotten what He first told us! The first thing Jonah discovered after the fish ejected him on dry land was that God's original message had not changed! "Go to the great city of Nineveh and proclaim to it the message I give you" (Jon. 3:2).

Have you been arguing with the Lord about His original orders to you? Have you hoped that, after all this time, the Lord has forgotten what He said or changed His mind? You should prepare for the sobering news that *nothing has changed.* God does not make idle comments when He speaks to us. He does not waste words. He makes no unguarded comments: "I the LORD do not change" (Mal. 3:6). "Every good and perfect gift is from above, coming down from the Father of the heavenly lights, who does not change like shifting shadows" (James 1:17). Don't try to change God's mind.

> How firm a foundation, ye saints of the Lord,
> Is laid for your faith in His excellent word!
> What more can He say than to you He hath said,
> You, who unto Jesus for refuge have fled?[1]
> —R. KEENE AND GEORGE KEITH

Martha might have surmised that the Lord was planning to raise her brother Lazarus from the dead. But she did not say what she was thinking or hoping. She merely pointed out how long Lazarus's body had been inside the cave and the awful odor that would be coming from it should they remove the stone. She might have said, "Lord, please raise Lazarus from the dead first, then I will have the stone removed. After all, if we can tell that he's in there walking around, I won't look stupid in front of all these people by doing the unthinkable thing of removing the stone."

God never asks us to do what we cannot do. Neither does He tend to do for us what we can do ourselves. Personally, I have learned this the hard way, then had Him withdraw, leaving me to work out things for myself. But I began to notice a pattern. When God worked in an extraordinary manner, it was because it was necessary at the time. My problem was that I wanted Him to continue doing everything—all the time!

For example, new converts often see unusual things happen in the first days or weeks after their coming to the Lord. Suddenly, without warning, the Lord seems to leave them, and they become discouraged. We all have had this happen. The Lord does for us what we cannot do; what we can do He expects us to do.

Martha could never have raised Lazarus from the dead, but she could remove the stone. That is all the Lord asked of her. All she had to do was to give consent to having it done!

But there was a price involved: her pride. She had to make an immediate choice in front of all who were watching— which included both believers and unbelievers. The choice was whether to expose herself by doing what Jesus asked, or to continue to argue with Him. It would have been far easier for her had only the two of them been standing near that cave.

God has a way of making us expose ourselves with people watching. Jesus said, "Whoever acknowledges me before men,

I will also acknowledge him before my Father in heaven. But whoever disowns me before men, I will disown him before my Father in heaven" (Matt. 10:32–33).

BELIEVE NOW, SEE LATER

One of the hardest things I ever did was to begin calling people forward after the Sunday night sermons when I was the pastor of Westminster Chapel in London. Going out into the streets, as I used to do, and talking to total strangers was far easier than giving an "appeal" in a church that had never practiced this. I used to say, "God, I will do it when You send great revival." It would not be difficult to do a thing like that when God was present in obvious power. What I wanted was for Jesus, as it were, to raise Lazarus from the dead from inside the tomb without having to remove the stone in front of everyone.

"Did I not tell you that if you believed, you would see the glory of God?" (John 11:40). Note the order: believing, then seeing. To those who insist on seeing before they expose themselves will be the abiding judgment of an *unchanged heart.* Seeing God's undoubted power and glory will not change the hearts of those who were only arguing about God. You may think that the raising of Lazarus from the dead would concern all who saw it. No. Some believed, yes. "But some of them went to the Pharisees and told them what Jesus had done" (John 11:46).

I can't prove it, but I dare say that those who were unconvinced after seeing Lazarus raised were the very ones who had said earlier, "Could not he who opened the eyes of the blind man have kept this man from dying?" (v. 37). I say this because Jesus said, "He that is faithful in that which is least is faithful also in much: and he that is *unjust* in the least is unjust also in much" (Luke 16:10, KJV, emphasis added). The raising of Lazarus would not have changed the hearts of those who only wanted to argue about God in the first place.

Argue with Him then, but not too much. Accept the rebuke, then get on with it. Expose yourself. Believe now; see later!

Martha opted for simple trust in Jesus's word. She gave her consent. "So they took away the stone..." (John 11:41). The Lord won the argument. But that made Martha the winner too.

God does not respond to those who argue about Him. I fear that much said by some ministers and theologians is argument *about* God rather than *for* God. So much talk nowadays that is theological sounds an awful lot like those from outside the family. I have a theological degree. I have been taught by some of the most erudite men in the world. I have listened to some of the most sophisticated lectures that can be heard. But the occasions on which I have heard someone speak at an academic level that made me feel he really *knew* God have been exceedingly rare. Apart from their desire sometimes to sound immensely learned, I have come away from so many lectures with the "gut" feeling that the speaker I just heard was almost as bitter toward God as those who said of Jesus, "Could not he who opened the eyes of the blind man have kept this man from dying?"

I have read theological monographs that, although claiming to defend God and speak for God, ended by supporting essentially the same arguments that professed atheists espoused. We used to call it atheism!

SEEK HIM

So much that takes place under the name of the church is little more than arguing about God. Ours is a day of discussions and conferences. There are always conferences going on somewhere—conferences about God. Many of these meet in order to see what can be done to bring people into the church. There will sometimes be an analysis of the latest survey. Sometimes these conferences will pray for God's blessing. But one fears that God responds in much the same way as our Lord did to those who wanted to accuse Him: silence.

What is needed more than anything else are not discussions about God, but talking *to* Him, wrestling *with* Him.

Have you ever wrestled with God? I recommend it; Jacob did. The result was that God gave him a new name—Israel. Once Jacob perceived that he was on the brink of being truly blessed from heaven, he wrestled all night, saying, "I will not let you go unless you bless me" (Gen. 32:26). He stayed with God, argued with Him, waited on Him, and would not give up until he found Him with an extraordinary assurance.

So can you. But don't stand aloof from God. Question your assumptions. Never, ever accuse Him; seek Him instead. Here is an infallible promise: "But if from there you seek the LORD your God, you will find him if you look for him with all your heart and with all your soul" (Deut. 4:29).

If you have a quarrel with God, then argue *with* Him, not *about* Him. He may rebuke you as He did Moses and Peter. But this is partly what is meant by wrestling with Him. The main thing is to talk with Him, stay on speaking terms with Him, and follow through with all His Word.

ARGUING *WITH* GOD

What, then, can be said about those who argue *with* God, as Martha did? The person who argues with God does so as a member of the family. Such a person is not on the outside looking in, but on the inside looking out. For this person has already been convinced that Jesus is the Son of God. Martha had earlier confessed this (John 11:27).

Confessing Jesus to be the Son of God, when it is done from the heart (which means you really do believe it), makes you a member of God's family at once. This does not mean you will not have questions. This does not mean you will not have doubts. It does not mean you will always understand the strange orders the Lord will give you—such as "Take away the stone," which prompted Martha's argument with Him.

The difference is that by being on the inside looking out, you continue to listen to the Lord. You look outside and see the same world that the non-Christian sees with all its suffering and sorrow, but you take your orders from the Lord as He speaks from within the family. You don't have all the answers. You even get orders sometimes that at first make no sense to you. But you listen to what the Lord says. Little by little you see that He has a perfect purpose in mind and gives you no idle directions. Any word from the Lord is precious, even when He tells one of us to remove the stone from a cave in which a dead body has lain for four days.

One crucial difference between Martha and those who wanted to accuse Jesus for letting Lazarus die is that Martha confessed Jesus to be the Son of God *without* having her questions answered. Those who stand aloof from God and are bent on accusing Him demand answers to their questions before they will "stoop" to faith. They feel that they are in a position to bargain with God. Some even feel that in their cleverness they have the "goods" on God, that they can, as it were, blackmail Him into answering their questions.

Those who demand answers to their questions before trusting the Lord Jesus Himself will not have their questions answered before faith comes. Faith alone leads to understanding. They will not be saved—or be given understanding—until they humble themselves and accept God's revelation of Himself in the Bible.

The irony is that Martha was a thousand times more heartbroken than those who stood aloof from Jesus and wanted to accuse Him. Martha was the one who originally couldn't understand why the Lord let Lazarus die.

It is not unusual that those who are in God's church and living for His glory have far greater heartaches than those in the world who just want to argue about God. Some of the world's greatest sufferers are in the family of God. They don't know *why* God allows their suffering. But they unashamedly confess Him as their Lord and Savior and keep on listening to Him. It was Job's wife who said, "Curse God and die!"

(Job 2:9), in the light of all the trouble that God allowed. His reply: "You are talking like a foolish woman. Shall we accept good from God, and not trouble?" (v. 10).

Those who argue with God from within His family do so because of needless fears. There are basically two fears that arise in our minds that tempt us to argue with the Lord. The first is the fear that the Lord won't recognize the obvious! No fear could be more groundless, and yet we tend to fear that God will not be aware of the most obvious things. "But, Lord," said Martha, "by this time there is a bad odor, for he has been there four days." As if Jesus did not know or hadn't thought of that!

TAKE GOD SERIOUSLY—HE KNOWS EVERYTHING

Sometimes we tend to argue with God about the most obvious things, as if He were stupid and needed to have a little light shed on the ordinary things of life. As I look back on my own life, I often find myself blushing that I argued with Him over certain things. It is as though we insult His intelligence.

God knows *everything*. Jesus said, "And even the very hairs of your head are all numbered" (Matt. 10:30). When we have the slightest hurt, He knows it. I have known the incredible joy of seeing God step in during my time of agony, doing so in such a manner that I was almost made speechless by His perfect timing. God is never too late, never too early, but always just on time. God knows all that is going on in the world generally, and with His loved ones particularly. He knows when I am lonely. He knows when I feel betrayed by a friend. He knows when I have financial pressure on me. He knows when I am feeling depressed. He knows when I am prone to anxiety. He knows when I am dreading certain things on the morrow. Our fear is that the Lord won't recognize the obvious.

The second fear that comes to the Christian is that the Lord has no plan of His own. When Martha was plainly told by Jesus, "Take away the stone" (John 11:39), she thought that the Lord made an unguarded comment. She may have thought that He was nervously making idle conversation since He had been weeping. When the Lord makes Himself real, almost vulnerable, to us, there is a danger of our being too familiar with Him. Normally Martha would not speak as she did to Jesus. But with Jesus weeping as He did, He seemed right on her level. Worst of all, she had no idea that the Lord had something in mind from the very moment He sent word that Lazarus's sickness was not "unto death" (v. 4, KJV).

When Jesus told her to take away the stone, He was proceeding according to plan. It is the devil who sneaks up on our blind side and suggests that God is leading us at random. The devil makes us think that the Lord isn't sure Himself what He's doing—like a television soap opera written a week at a time because writers and producers need to wait for a little feedback from the audience before they carry on too far.

Nothing gives me more courage than the realization that God has a plan for my life. He is in the process of leading me from A to Z. I don't know what Z is, therefore I wait for the knowledge of what B is. I am often asked, "Can we avoid God's will?" I answer, "Only if we *want* to avoid it." Jonah wanted to avoid God's will (Jon. 1:3). But the end of Jonah's story convinces me that Jonah both avoided and also did not avoid God's will. Nothing took God by surprise. God knew what Jonah's reaction would be to the initial news that he must go to Nineveh. I suspect that God began preparing Jonah's fish even before Jonah disobeyed.

Samson is an example of a man who apparently avoided God's will. He foolishly let Delilah talk him into sharing the secret of his great strength (Judg. 16:17). There was no more pathetic figure than Samson in the days following such an awful downfall, but in the end we discover that Samson accomplished more by his death, in terms of defeating Israel's enemies, than in the whole of this life (Judg. 16:30). He was even referred to in the great "faith" chapter of the Bible (Heb. 11:32).

God looks after His family. After all, He sent His one and only Son into the world to bring "many sons to glory" (Heb. 2:10). Those sons are adopted sons (Rom. 8:15; Gal. 4:6; Eph. 1:5). Jesus was God's only "natural" Son. The rest of us have been brought into God's family by adoption. As adopted sons, moreover, we are made "co-heirs with Christ" (Rom. 8:17). This means that I am called to inherit all that Jesus will inherit. This is because *God loves us as much as He loves Jesus.* I know of no more dazzling thought. I base this statement not only on Romans 8:17 but also on John 17:23, where our Lord prayed for us: "...that you sent me and have loved them [that is, us] even as you have loved me [that is, Jesus]." Therefore God loves us as much as He loves His only Son, and He looks after us as He did His Son. This means He plans for us as He did for His Son. Paul said that he knelt "before the Father, from whom his whole family in heaven and on earth derives its name," that through Him we may receive "immeasurably more than all we ask or imagine" (Eph. 3:14, 20). All because we are a part of His family.

Martha would not have argued with the Lord as she did had she stopped to realize that the Lord always has a plan for His loved ones. Is the Lord asking you to do something that seems as odd as taking the stone away from a cave in which a four-day-old corpse has lain? Have you said, "But, Lord, You know I can't do *that*"?

Whenever the Lord says something to us—however strange and unreasonable it may seem—remember that He has something "up His sleeve"! All you need do is take Him seriously.

10

DOES JESUS CARE WHEN WE HAVE NO FAITH?

There comes a moment in time when God lets us know what He has been doing. This is true for His church—His family—and it is true for each of us individually.

The Lord knows how much we can bear. He tests our faith, sometimes to the limit, but never beyond our ability to cope. "No temptation [or trial] has seized you except what is common to man. And God is faithful; he will not let you be tempted [or tested] beyond what you can bear" (1 Cor. 10:13). It is helpful to know that the Greek word *peirasmos* is translated either as "temptation" or "trial," and the context determines which was intended. In 1 Corinthians 10:13, there is no doubt that either translation fits.

God is never too early, never too late, but always just on time. He sometimes appears none too soon! But He always comes when we need Him most.

God had a plan for Lazarus, Martha, Mary, and all of us by Lazarus's illness and subsequent death. As soon as Jesus had word of Lazarus's illness, I suspect the Father immediately let Him see the plan from A to Z. As we have seen, it was even a test for Jesus to follow through with the Father's plan. He had to keep from telling everyone what He was doing. All Jesus did from the moment He heard that Lazarus was ill came by deliberate design.

GOD'S WILL—BELIEVE IT OR NOT

All that can be grasped in our story of Lazarus and his sisters can be summarized under the heading of the secret will of God. God has a purpose that is known only to Himself. It is hidden from us. That is why we call it secret. It is not unknown to Him. He knows exactly what He will do, but it is hidden from us.

There is another equally important aspect of God's will that is known as His revealed will. This refers to His plain commands and teachings. It is summarized by Paul in one word: *love*. For love fulfills the law. That is, if you will live by love, you will keep every one of the Ten Commandments (Rom. 13:8–10).

The love Paul speaks of is *agape* love that is depicted in the New Testament as selfless concern. It was the love that motivated God to send His Son into the world (John 3:16), and it is the love Paul is describing in the famous "love" chapter— 1 Corinthians 13. It is not *eros* love (physical love) or *philia* love (brotherly or family love). It is an unselfish concern for all. Jesus said, "A new command I give you: Love one another. As I have loved you, so you must love one another" (John 13:34). That is God's revealed will to us.

God's will, then, is to be understood as either His secret will or His revealed will. Most of us are far more interested in God's secret will than in His revealed will. All of us are more interested in what God is doing than we are in what our responsibility is. We want to know such things as: Is it God's will for me to have this job? Will I be able to go on this holiday? Will I get well? Will I get married, and if so, to whom? Will revival really come to our church? What is His will for my future?

I believe that we should believe equally in both God's secret will and His revealed will. If we don't have a firm grasp that God does have a will of His own for us (but which is secret), we shall have no vision of His sovereignty and His eternal purpose generally. If we don't have a firm conviction that we are to obey His revealed will, we shall become passive and indifferent, if not fatalistic. This would be dangerous. If pressed to say which is more important, I would say it is God's revealed will. For this is our responsibility. The secret will of God is His responsibility. To put it another way, the secret will of God will be revealed in time, whether we believe in it or not!

The revealed will of God in one word is this: the Bible. If you want to know what God's will is, read the Bible. He has a secret will for every one of us, but there is no way we can know what it is before we have obeyed what is plainly stated in His Word.

Martha would never have known what God's secret purpose was (to raise Lazarus) until she obeyed (agreed to remove the stone). Obeying the revealed will of God will eventually bring us to see clearly what the secret will of God is. But remember the order: revealed will, secret will. Obey and you will eventually know.

Perhaps the best illustration to the secret and revealed will of God pertains to the second coming of Jesus. I believe that Jesus is coming soon. But only a fool would say that he *knows* Jesus is coming soon, not to say when He will come. No one knows that. That is secret. God knows. We don't. Jesus said, "No one knows about that day or hour, not even the angels in heaven, nor the Son, but only the Father" (Mark 13:32). What is God's revealed will with regard to our Lord's second coming? That we are ready for it! "So you also must be ready, because the Son of Man will come at an hour when you do not expect him" (Matt. 24:44).

God's Will (His Plan) for You

Maybe you are not a Christian but you would very much like to know what God's will is for you. I can tell you: to become a Christian, to be born again, and to be converted. This is His revealed will. God is "not willing that any should perish, but that all should come to repentance" (2 Pet. 3:9, KJV). God "wants all men to be saved and to come to a knowledge of the truth" (1 Tim. 2:4). You cannot possibly know God's secret will concerning yourself until you have met the first requirement God makes of you: to acknowledge Jesus Christ as your

Savior and Lord, to repent of your sins, and to trust the blood that Jesus shed on the cross.

After a person becomes a Christian, the next question that should be asked is: how is the Christian life to be lived? I have in fact already answered that: by the law of love. But there is another important verse in this connection: "But if we walk in the light, as he is in the light, we have fellowship with one another, and the blood of Jesus, his Son, purifies us from all sin" (1 John 1:7). The cleansing blood of Jesus is to be a daily experience. After conversion, one must walk in the light, read the Bible daily, and be open to the Holy Spirit at all times. He will show you things you need to know (Phil. 3:15).

What you don't know you don't need to know. What you *don't* know is God's secret will. What you *do* know is what He has revealed. Always follow the revealed will of God.

You will also eventually be able to know something of the impulse of the Spirit. But remember that any impulse of the Spirit will not lead you contrary to what is plainly revealed in the Bible. The Bible was given to us not to replace the impulse of the Spirit, but partly to correct error and abuses that relate to divine guidance. The leadership of the Holy Spirit will *never* conflict with the revealed will of God that is *agape* love and walking in the light.

Are you wondering at the moment what God is working in your own life? Have you been perplexed in the light of a series of inexplicable events? Are you tempted to vacillate between leaning on what you *know* is true (that Jesus cares) and what you nonetheless find bewildering (His delay in coming to your rescue)?

Has it crossed your mind that God just might be doing something *big*? I do not want to mislead you here. I do not want to present a false hope before you and cause you to look forward to something that is but illusory. And yet, there is a way that we can discern the "signs of the times."

When certain Pharisees and Sadducees tried to test Jesus by asking Him for a sign from heaven, He replied, "When evening comes, you say, 'It will be fair weather, for the sky is red,' and in the morning, 'Today it will be stormy, for the sky is red and overcast.' You know how to interpret the appearance of the sky, but you cannot interpret the signs of the times" (Matt. 16:2–3). What He meant by "the signs of the times" does not refer merely to cosmic, eschatological events. The signs are also referring to God's timing and purpose to break through to us individually in a most marvelous manner.

SIGNS OF BEYOND THE ORDINARY

What are the signs that God may be on the brink of doing something beyond the ordinary in our lives? If we let the story of Lazarus and his two sisters be our pattern, there are ten signs that will bear out examination from John 11. Here is the pattern:

1. *Urgent need.* "Lord, the one you love is sick" (v. 3). The first hint that God is going to do something unusual is the emergence of urgent need. It many not be a physical ailment. It could be a financial crisis, a marriage crisis, an abrupt change in life, a severe trial, a sudden betrayal,

a complete reversal in the predictability of things you had taken for granted. But it is quite sudden—and urgent. If so, this qualifies for the possibility that God is up to something big in your life.

2. *Seeking the Lord.* "So the sisters sent word to Jesus" (v. 3). The first thing that Martha and Mary did was to seek the Lord. They called on His name. They sent word to Jesus. This means prayer. My own father sometimes called it "sending a telegram to heaven." Sometimes you have to do it in a split second. You may not even have time to get on your knees or bow your head, not to mention call on your pastor, minister, or close friend. You are boxed in with no choice but to turn directly and urgently to God. Do it!

> O what peace we often forfeit,
> O what needless pain we bear,
> All because we do not carry
> Everything to God in prayer.[1]
> —Joseph M. Scriven

3. *A veiled encouragement.* "This sickness is not unto death" (v. 4, KJV). When Jesus heard of Lazarus's illness, He sent a word back to the three of them. "This sickness is not unto death, but for the glory of God, that the Son of God might be glorified thereby" (v. 4, KJV). That

word spelled encouragement, regardless of whatever else it may have meant to them when they heard it. I don't think they knew all that it meant. But it could only have encouraged them. Any word from the Lord is encouraging. When the Lord is doing something unusual He gives encouragement and makes us feel better—even if we don't know exactly why.

4. *The hiding of God's face.* "...he stayed where he was two more days" (v. 6). This is when God first lets Himself be misunderstood. It hurts Him to do it because He loves you. God is so tender. Did you not know this about God? "The Lord is very pitiful, and of tender mercy" (James 5:11, kjv). Whenever He hides His face, it grieves Him; it hurts Him. It is much like when you, as a parent, have to show displeasure with a child. You just show by your facial expression that you are unhappy. But there is a difference between just any parent and our perfect parent, God the Father: we tend to be provoked by our children about something they have done already, and God hides His face as a preventative measure. Therefore we cannot see why God would hide His face at the time. It is because God is looking ahead. When this happens we must not be quick to take it personally and begin accusing ourselves: "Oh, what have I done?" When you

have to ask, "What have I done?" it is probably true that you have done nothing in particular that caused the Lord to hide Himself. He may have no "reason" to hide His face in reaction to what we have done. He just does it, yet He has a reason: He is looking beyond.

5. *Things go from bad to worse.* "So then he told them plainly, 'Lazarus is dead'...'Lord,' Martha said to Jesus, 'if you had been here, my brother would not have died'" (John 11:14, 21). When things go from bad to worse, it is a very good sign indeed that God is doing something special. He does not allow things to happen that would ultimately demoralize us. What He allows is to bring us to the place whereby God alone would be the explanation for any good. God loves to bring us to the place where things appear beyond any hope and when the outlook is sheer bleakness. God loves to have to handle matters which, humanly speaking, spell "too late." "For nothing is impossible with God" (Luke 1:37).

6. *Being brought to tears.* "Jesus saw her weeping" (John 11:33). Have you been brought to tears? Have you been broken yet? Has this not been your need? Perhaps you have needed mellowing and refining that could only come about through tears. Could it be that God

wanted to bring His family to tears before they could see the glory of God? Could it be that He postpones the unveiling of His glory because we are too hard and cold? *"They that sow in tears shall reap in joy. He that goeth forth and weepeth,* bearing precious seed, shall doubtless come again with rejoicing, bringing his sheaves with him"* (Ps. 126:5–6, KJV, emphasis added).

7. *Seeing that Jesus does care after all.* "Jesus wept. Then the Jews said, 'See how he loved him!'" (John 11:35–36). One needs to see sooner or later that Jesus does indeed have feelings and that He has been involved all along, even when He appeared not to care. But before we see God work, there is a need on our part to see clearly how much God cares. In Dr. O. S. Hawkins's remarkable book *Tracing the Rainbow through the Rain,* there emerges the clear picture of how much God is, in fact, in touch with the world and those He loves.[2] As long as we think that God does not care, the devil can walk all over us as we moan helplessly. But once we are given to see, with objectivity, how much the Lord really feels and how deeply He cares, we are transformed at once into a state of expectancy by which faith works unhindered. This is what ensures Satan's defeat.

8. *The call for obedience in the small things.* "Take
    away the stone" (v. 39). The small things always
    seem great at first, however. This is what makes
    obedience in what is least so daunting. Yet what
    is presented to us as B—for God always leads
    from A to B, not directly from A to Z—seems
    very challenging indeed. God never asks us to
    do what we cannot do, and He does not put
    more on us than we can bear. When He gives
    orders, it is because we can take them and
    carry them out, for around the corner is that
    which only God can carry out. But to prepare
    us for the unveiling of His glory and power, He
    leads us by the hand and gives us orders along
    the way.

9. *Carrying out obedience in the small things.* "So
    they took away the stone" (v. 41). If we are not
    obedient in the small things, we shall not only
    be disobedient in the big things, but we also
    won't get to *enjoy* big things at all. We won't
    progress further in God's plan until we do what
    we are indeed able to do. Are you waiting on
    God to do what you yourself could do? Is there
    something staring you in the face that you
    know in your heart is your own responsibility?
    You may say, "But God is able to do that for me."
    Yes, that is true. Jesus could have walked over
    and removed the stone for Martha, but He told

her to do it. Once the Lord gives an order, He will not proceed further until we have carried it out. The Lord will not do for you what He has told you to do. You must do it before anything else will happen.

10. *The Lord takes over completely.* "Then Jesus looked up and said, 'Father, I thank you that you have heard me. I knew that you always hear me, but I said this for the benefit of the people standing here, that they may believe that you sent me.' When he had said this, Jesus called in a loud voice, 'Lazarus, come out!' The dead man came out, his hands and feet wrapped with strips of linen, and a cloth around his face" (vv. 41–44).

There comes a time at which we can go no further. There comes a moment when there is nothing more we can do; no more obedience is called for—only a turning over of things to the Lord. He then takes over completely. Once we have carried out the last act of obedience, the Lord says, "All right. Leave it to Me." Peter called it, "Casting all your care upon him; for he careth for you" (1 Pet. 5:7, KJV).

THE INTERCESSORY WORK OF JESUS

The first thing the Lord does when He steps in and takes complete control is to intercede. "Then Jesus looked up and said, 'Father, I thank you that you have heard me'" (John 11:41). Normally we should not be given visible access to this intercessory work of Jesus Christ. It is what goes on secretly between the Father and the Son. This is partly why Jesus said, "I said this for the benefit of the people standing here" (v. 42). What happened near Lazarus's tomb is what is always going on at the right hand of God. We were given a glimpse of it at the tomb of Lazarus.

Jesus is now at the right hand of God. What is He doing there? He is "interceding for us" (Rom. 8:34), says Paul. He saves those "who come to God through him, because he always lives to intercede for them" (Heb. 7:25).

But if we are to learn from our Lord's way of handling Martha at Lazarus's tomb, we should not presume that He does intercede until we have done what He has told us to do. I do not say that there is no intercession on our behalf at other times (I am sure that it is going on all the time). But the picture that the Holy Spirit provides for us is that of our Lord taking over once we have done everything. "After you have done everything, to stand" (Eph. 6:13).

There comes a time when there is nothing else to do but wait. "Do not be afraid. Stand firm and you will see the deliverance the LORD will bring you today. . . . *The LORD will fight for you;* you need only to be still" (Exod. 14:13–14, emphasis added).

One morning I was driving in my car from Palmer to Nashville, Tennessee. I had been in a crisis for days, feeling nothing but anxiety, but having no idea what was the Lord's will. I decided to spend the time in prayer as I drove on the old U.S. Highway 41. I had just come to the bottom of Mount Eagle in southeastern Tennessee. Praying with the most intense agony as I drove, I began to think of two verses: "For my yoke is easy and my burden is light" (Matt. 11:30), and "Casting all your care upon him; for he careth for you" (1 Pet. 5:7, KJV). I began to pray that the Lord would help me to cast all of my care on Him.

In a few moments there came, unexpectedly, an almost visible access to the Lord's intercessory work at God's right hand. I suppose you would have to call it a vision, but it seemed at the time as though I was taken right into the immediate presence of God. All I know is that the Lord Jesus was praying for me—I mean He was, as it were, identifying Himself with me. I never dreamed that the Lord cared so much. I could see that not only was He fully aware of all my anxiety, but He loved me more than I loved myself. Tears flowed down my face as I continued to drive. When I get to heaven I am going to ask for a video replay of that morning of October 31, 1955.

I wonder now how I was able to drive through various Tennessee cities and towns. The next thing I remember was passing through a little town called Smyrna nearly an hour later. I entered into a rest of the soul that gave me a peace and sense of God's glory beyond anything I thought possible in this present life. I can say categorically that on that morning—and it lasted for days—Jesus was more real to me than any*one* else or any*thing* else. I saw His glory. It was what God has been up to all along. But once I sensed that the Lord was interceding for me, I became merely a spectator. I literally enjoyed seeing Him take over.

Conversion: Life From the Dead

"Then Jesus looked up and said, 'Father…'" (John 11:41). Once the Lord does that, all we need to do is watch and, if anything, just stay out of the way.

After Jesus finished praying He called in a loud voice, "Lazarus, come out!" It has been observed by many that if Jesus had not singled out Lazarus, every tomb within a mile or two would have burst asunder with the dead rising forth! But He singled out Lazarus. He called him by name. What joy it was for Jesus to do that!

Lazarus raised from the dead is a picture of true conversion. For all of us are born spiritually dead. Born dead. "As for you, you were dead in your transgressions and sins" (Eph. 2:1). We can witness to the lost, pray for our loved ones, do all within our own strength to see people saved, but unless the Lord Jesus steps in and calls us by name, we shall remain as helpless and hopeless as any dead person.

Conversion is literally life from the dead. It is what God does.

Some conversions are more spectacular than others, but, in every case, it is necessary for the Lord to bring it about. Whether conversion is the more extraordinary like that of Saul of Tarsus (Acts 9:1–22), or the more ordinary like that of Lydia, "whose heart the Lord opened" (Acts 16:14, KJV), "salvation comes from the LORD" (Jon. 2:9).

SAVING FAITH, BUT WEAK EXPERIMENTAL FAITH

Does Jesus care if we have no faith? There are four categories that pertain to faith in our present account of the raising of Lazarus. First, there was the *presence of a saving faith, but a weak experimental faith*. That was Martha's faith. What is "saving" faith? It is the faith that saves. It is the faith by which you know you are saved and you will go to heaven when you die.

Is there such a thing as a faith that is not "saving"? Yes. There is mere intellectual faith. The devil has that kind of faith. The devil is not an atheist. "You believe that there is one God. Good! Even the demons believe that—and shudder" (James 2:19). Intellectual faith is believing certain things to be true, but without trust in what Jesus Christ has done for you. You believe in the Apostles' Creed? Good! But so does anyone with mere intellectual faith.

There is also a temporal, or crisis, faith. This is turning to God when you are in a crisis.

In war many in the military would call on God to preserve their lives. But when the war was over they didn't need God anymore. You can do the same thing with your temporal needs—pray when you are unwell or need special guidance. But it is not saving faith. You could even have your prayers answered and be lost and go on to hell.

Saving faith is when you transfer all trust that you have had in yourself to what Jesus has done for you. It is doing this from your heart. It is believing and confessing that Jesus is the Son of God. This is the faith that Martha had (John 11:27).

But Martha had a weak "experimental" faith. Experimental faith—putting things to the test—is truly believing that things will happen here below. Saving faith will get you to heaven. Experimental faith sees things happen in the here and now. Martha believed that God *was able* to raise Lazarus from the dead (v. 22), but she doubted whether Jesus *was going to do it.*

Some Christians never move much beyond their own saving faith. They believe the Lord will save them. They are Christians. But when it comes to believing that God will do the extraordinary, they have no faith whatsoever.

Yet Martha did give consent for the stone to be removed. She was listening to the Lord and obeying Him. But she was weak in experimental faith.

THOSE WHO HAD NOT YET BELIEVED

The second category of people present at Lazarus's tomb was *those who had not yet believed by whom they could be saved.* This may have been those who said of Jesus, "See how he loved him!" (v. 36). I can't be sure, but it is likely that they were the ones described immediately after Jesus raised Lazarus: "Therefore many of the Jews who had come to visit Mary, and had seen what Jesus did, put their faith in him" (v. 45). It would seem from this that they were not believers at first. Their openness as Jesus began to walk toward Lazarus's tomb may have stood them in good stead. It is important to remain open and uncritical.

Perhaps this second category described you as you began reading this book. Perhaps by now you have been converted.

If so, that is entirely the work of the Holy Spirit. It was the sovereign providence of God that put this book into your hands in the first place. If you have followed along without being hostile, be thankful for such overruling grace from God. For by nature we are all hostile to God. Jonathan Edwards had a sermon called "Men Naturally Are God's Enemies" that equally shows how God feels about you![3] You are under His wrath (John 3:36; Eph. 2:3). It is therefore of His great mercy that you are spared (Eph. 2:4). If indeed you have been open to the Lord, it would not be surprising if you have already opened your heart to Him—which means the Lord opened your heart!

But if you are wondering how exactly a person becomes a Christian, here is a prayer you can pray (do it now):

> *Dear God, I know that I am a sinner. I am sorry for my sins. I believe that Jesus is the Son of God. I believe He died on the cross for my sins. Wash my sins away by His blood. I welcome Your Holy Spirit into my life. As best as I know how, I give You my life. In Jesus's name, amen.*

If you prayed that prayer and meant it with all your heart, you are there—you're saved. Whether you particularly "feel" anything does not matter. What matters is whether you meant—and continue to mean—what you prayed. You need to share this with another person—soon. It may be the person who gave you this book. But tell at least one other person what has happened to you. Jesus said, "Verily, verily, I say unto you, He that believeth on me hath everlasting life"

(John 6:47, KJV). I ask you this: *if* that word of Jesus *is* absolutely true and you *were* to die today, where would you go? Answer: heaven. That is where I would go, and I make this claim not on my good works, but on *Jesus's own Word*. He did not say, "He that worketh hath everlasting life." No. It is faith. "For it is by grace you have been saved, through faith—and this not from yourselves, it is the gift of God—not by works, so that no one can boast" (Eph. 2:8–9).

THOSE WHO HAD NO FAITH

The third category present at Lazarus's tomb was *those who had no faith and who would apparently be lost.* They were those we have examined a number of times in this book, who said, "Could not he who opened the eyes of the blind man have kept this man from dying?" (John 11:37). They were those who were detached from what Jesus was up to and remained aloof from any direct contact with Him. They were the ones who wanted to argue about God and do so by accusing Him for letting Lazarus die in the first place.

Those who remain in this hostile state when they are confronted with the living Christ often stay that way.

There was a wonderful exception, however: Saul of Tarsus. None could have been more hostile toward the Lord Jesus Christ than Saul of Tarsus. He had permission from the high priest in Jerusalem to arrest Christians. He was on his way to Damascus to arrest some more when, "As he neared Damascus on his journey, suddenly a light from heaven flashed around him. He fell to the ground and heard a voice say to him, 'Saul,

Saul, why do you persecute me?' 'Who are you, Lord?' Saul asked. 'I am Jesus, whom you are persecuting,' he replied" (Acts 9:3–5).

As a consequence of this, Saul turned to the Lord and eventually became the great apostle Paul. He later wrote: "Even though I was once a blasphemer and a persecutor and a violent man, I was shown mercy because I acted in ignorance and unbelief" (1 Tim. 1:13).

What worries me about those who scoffed at Lazarus's tomb, however, was not only the way they talked *before* Lazarus was raised, but also *after.* One would have thought it would be impossible not to believe in Jesus after He raised Lazarus from the dead, especially if one saw it all happen. But for some it made no difference.

Although some (as we have seen) believed, "Some of them went to the Pharisees and told them what Jesus had done" (John 11:46). This in fact led to Jesus's arrest, trial, and crucifixion. I think it is highly likely that those who did not put their trust in Jesus after the raising of Lazarus were the same ones who had the hostile attitude from the beginning.

Perfect: The Faith of Jesus

The fourth category that pertains to faith that was present at Lazarus's tomb was that of a *perfect faith: the faith of Jesus.* There had to be a perfect faith somewhere, or Lazarus would never have been raised. There wasn't a person anywhere who would have looked toward that open cave and shouted,

"Lazarus, come out!" but our Lord Jesus Christ. He took things in hand because He alone had the faith to raise the dead.

Does Jesus care when we have no faith? Yes. How did He show it? By requiring no more of them than what they could do. When Martha agreed to have the stone removed, she had reached the zenith of her strength. Our Lord does not impose demands on us that are unrealistic. Once Martha had done that, Jesus turned to the Father and never again turned to anyone present.

This is why we are justified by His faith (Gal. 2:16). Our own faith is in Him—His faith, His obedience, His work, His blood. Jesus paid it all!

> I hear the Saviour say,
> "Thy strength indeed is small;
> Child of weakness, watch and pray,
> Find in Me thine all in all."
>
> For nothing good have I
> Whereby Thy grace to claim,
> I'll wash my garments white
> In the blood of Calv'ry's Lamb.
>
> Jesus paid it all,
> All to Him I owe;
> Sin had left a crimson stain,
> He washed it white as snow.[4]
>
> —ELVINA MABEL HALL

TO INCREASE OUR FAITH

The pattern that emerges from the story of Jesus, Lazarus, and the two sisters is repeated all the time. God is always leading us by the hand to show His glory. We are always being changed "from glory to glory" (2 Cor. 3:18, KJV). The revelation of what God had in mind leads us directly into another era, during which we are again made to trust Him.

Perhaps the key statement of Jesus in this whole account was, "For your sake I am glad I was not there, so that you may believe" (John 11:15). God lets things that we don't understand happen for one reason: to increase our faith.

God is always leading us to more glory. The greater the battle, the greater the victory. The deeper the misunderstanding, the higher the revelation of His will and purpose. It is all worth waiting for. "No eye has seen, no ear has heard, no mind has conceived what God has prepared for those who love him" (1 Cor. 2:9).

Does Jesus care? Yes, He cares. All that He is doing is designed ultimately to show not only that He cares, but also how much He cares. He does not tell us at first what He is up to. He makes us wait. When Jesus was hanging on the cross, no one understood it. "How can this be?" they thought. How could a man who could rebuke a storm and bring instant calm now be hanging helplessly on a cross? How could one who walked on water be dying? How could one who raised Lazarus from the dead be in such a pitiful state? But there He was—bleeding, dying.

He never told anyone what its purpose was. For example, He never called Peter to one side to say, "Now, Peter, here is what is going to happen. I am going to die on a cross. It will be for the sins of the world. I will be raised on the third day. It is all for the purpose of accomplishing salvation." Jesus never explained why He would die on a cross. It was the best-kept secret in the world. Satan thought he had pulled off the greatest coup that ever was. But it guaranteed his defeat instead. "None of the rulers of this age understood it, for if they had, they would not have crucified the Lord of glory" (1 Cor. 2:8).

HE HAS A PLAN

Whenever we are disappointed in the Lord's reaction to our request, know that He has a better idea in mind.

What about the evil and suffering in the world? Does He care? If so, will He show it?

He will. I don't know how, but He will. There is coming a day when God will clear His name. He will answer those who asked, "Could not he who opened the eyes of the blind man have kept this man from dying?" He will answer those who say, "Where was God when I needed Him?"

Disappointed though Martha and Mary were for a while, do you think they had any quarrel with Jesus by the time He showed what He had in mind?

To those who cannot abide a God who allows evil and suffering I offer this counsel: let us lower our voices. Wait. God is all wise. He has a plan. When it is wholly revealed, every mouth will be stopped. If I may give what may be thought as a naïve, if not crude, illustration, it is like one end of an ingenious spy story. My favorite writer is John le Carré. He has a way of writing so that you cannot fully grasp what is going on until you come to the very end. Then it all falls into place. It is done in such a manner that the reader says, "Ah, yes. Why didn't I think of that? I should have seen it all along." But a master author like le Carré is able to keep the meaning hidden from the reader until the very end.

How much more so with God! When He clears His name on the last day and answers all our questions, we will bow and worship. And we will see how clearly God was at work all along to show that He cares.

WHOSOEVER BELIEVETH ON HIM

Neither does this mean that all will be happy in the end. The Bible teaches that there will be those eternally lost. But they will know that God is holy and righteous. They will gnash their teeth because of their realization of God's just ways with the world He made. He has already said that all men are "without excuse" (Rom. 1:20). On the last day they will admit it openly.

In the meantime let us be content with the words of the prophet Isaiah: "'For my thoughts are not your thoughts, neither are your ways my ways,' declares the LORD. 'As the heavens are higher than the earth, so are my ways higher than your ways and my thoughts than your thoughts'" (Isa. 55:8–9).

To those who will take these words to heart there will inevitably come great peace. "Whosoever believeth on him shall not be ashamed" (Rom. 10:11, KJV).

God is doing something in your own life. His delays are hints that He has something better in mind for you than your ideas. Wait and see. Believe and see. Whatever is happening at the moment, you can be sure of this: it is for the glory of God. "Vengeance is mine" (Rom. 12:19, KJV). His way of vindicating is a thousand times better than your way, even if you had a thousand years to plan it. It is exciting to know that God loves to vindicate, and even more wonderful to see how He does it!

"Lord, if you had been here, my brother would not have died." That is true. Neither would Lazarus have been raised from the dead, which was a far better idea.

It is the same for you. Why? Because Jesus cares.

NOTES

INTRODUCTION

1. "Does Jesus Care" by Frank E. Graeff. Public domain.

CHAPTER 1
DOES JESUS CARE WHEN WE ARE UNWELL?

1. "What a Friend We Have in Jesus" by Joseph M. Scriven. Public domain.

CHAPTER 3
DOES JESUS CARE WHEN WE ARE AFRAID?

1. "Amazing Grace" by John Newton. Public domain.

CHAPTER 4
DOES JESUS CARE WHEN WE MISUNDERSTAND HIM?

1. "Were You There," African American spiritual. Author unknown. Public domain.
2. ThinkExist.com, "Saint Augustine Quotes," http://thinkexist .com/quotation/thou-hast-made-us-for-thyself-o-lord-and -our/347709.html (accessed January 31, 2008).

CHAPTER 5
DOES JESUS CARE WHEN WE BLAME HIM?

1. "He Died for Me" by John Newton. Public domain.
2. "Jesus the Very Thought of Thee" by Bernard of Clairvaux, translated from Latin to English by Edward Caswall, Lyra Catholica. Public domain.

CHAPTER 6
DOES JESUS CARE WHEN WE
ACKNOWLEDGE HIS POWER?

1. "The Solid Rock" by Edward Mote. Public domain.
2. J. I. Packer, *Knowing God,* rev. ed. (Downers Grove, IL: InterVarsity Press, 1973).

CHAPTER 7
DOES JESUS CARE WHEN WE
ACKNOWLEDGE HIS DEITY?

1. Dale Carnegie, *How to Win Friends and Influence People* (New York: Simon and Schuster, 1936). Reprinted with preface by Dorothy Carnegie (New York: Pocket Books, a division of Simon & Schuster, Inc., 1982).
2. "Pass Me Not" by Fanny Jane Crosby. Public domain.

CHAPTER 8
DOES JESUS CARE WHEN WE CRY?

1. Everett L. Shostrom, *Man, the Manipulator* (New York: Bantam Books, 1968, 1980).
2. "Standing Somewhere in the Shadows" by E. J. Rollings, copyright © 1947 Word Music, LLC (a div. of Word Music Group, Inc.). Permission applied for from Music Services.
3. "He Helps Us Through" by Floyd W. Hawkins, copyright © 1936. Copyright renewed 1964 Lillenas Publishing Company (admin. by The Copyright Company). Permission applied for from The Copyright Company.

CHAPTER 9
DOES JESUS CARE WHEN WE ARGUE WITH HIM?

1. "How Firm a Foundation" by R. Keene and George Keith. Public domain.

CHAPTER 10
DOES JESUS CARE WHEN WE HAVE NO FAITH?

1. "What a Friend We Have in Jesus" by Joseph M. Scriven. Public domain.

2. O. S. Hawkins, *Tracing the Rainbow Through the Rain* (Nashville: B&H Publishing Group, 1985).

3. The Jonathan Edwards Collection—Bible Bulletin Board, "Men Naturally Are God's Enemies," http://www.biblebb.com/edwards.htm (accessed November 15, 2007).

4. "Jesus Paid It All" by Elvina Mabel Hall. Public domain.

If you have found encouragement from

The Unfailing Love of Jesus

here is another book we think

you will love.

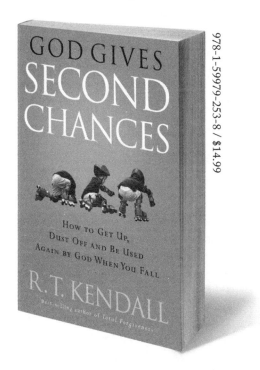

978-1-59979-253-8 / $14.99